Mary Charrington

Starter Teacher's Book

Contents

Syllabus	p.
Introduction	p.
Unit 1 teaching notes	p. 8
Unit 2 teaching notes	p. 12
Unit 3 teaching notes	p. 16
Unit 1–3 *Project time* and *Revision time* notes	p. 20
Unit 4 teaching notes	p. 21
Unit 5 teaching notes	p. 25
Unit 6 teaching notes	p. 29
Unit 4–6 *Project time* and *Revision time* notes	p. 33
Unit 7 teaching notes	p. 34
Unit 8 teaching notes	p. 37
Unit 9 teaching notes	p. 41
Unit 7–9 *Project time* and *Revision time* notes	p. 45
Unit 10 teaching notes	p. 46
Unit 11 teaching notes	p. 50
Unit 12 teaching notes	p. 54
Unit 10–12 *Project time* and *Revision time* notes	p. 58
Festivals teaching notes – Halloween	p. 59
Festivals teaching notes – Christmas	p. 60
Festivals teaching notes – Easter	p. 61
Special needs teaching notes	p. 62
Games bank	p. 64
Tests tapescripts and answer key	p. 65
Test 1	p. 66
Test 2	p. 68
Test 3	p. 70
Test 4	p. 72
Portfolio teaching notes	p. 74
Portfolio pages	p. 75
Wordlist	p. 79

New Chatterbox TB Starter Language Coverage

Unit	Language (structures)	Topic and vocabulary	Skills and functions
1	Hello / Hi, Goodbye I'm … Stand up, Sit down, Open your book, Close your book, Look, Listen	Greetings and introductions Classroom language	Saying Hello and Goodbye Introducing yourself Responding to classroom language
2	1–10 What's this? It's a … bag, pen, pencil, rubber, pencil case, book	Numbers 1–10 Classroom objects	Counting to 10 Identifying, naming, and asking about classroom objects
3	This is my … mum, dad, sister, brother Who's this? My …	Members of the family	Identifying, naming, and asking about members of the family
Project time! Revision time! My school/ My family Revision	Revision: This is my … family, classroom	Classroom objects Members of the family	Identifying with another culture Playing an oral game to practise vocabulary
4	white, green, yellow, black, red, blue Happy Birthday! How old are you? I'm …	Colours Revision: Numbers	Identifying and naming colours Asking someone's age Saying how old you are
5	Is it a …? Yes / No ball, car, teddy bear, doll, bike, guitar Revision: What's this? It's a …	Toys	Identifying, naming and asking about toys
6	What colour is it? It's … purple, brown, pink, orange, grey	More colours	Identifying, naming and asking about colours
Project time! Revision time! My birthday Revision	Here's … It's a … It's fantastic! How old are you? I'm …	Birthdays General revision	Identifying with another culture Playing an oral game to practise vocabulary
7	I'm / You're / She's / He's … big, small, hungry, thirsty, sad, happy	Adjectives	Using adjectives to describe yourself and others

8	I've got a ... hamster, rabbit, cat, dog, bird, fish Revision: This is my ...	Animals	Identifying, naming and talking about pets Talking about owning pets Describing pets using colour words
9	Have you got a / an ...? Yes / No a sandwich, a sausage, an apple, an orange, a donut Revision: I've got a ...	Food	Identifying, naming and asking about food
Project time! **Revision time!** My pets	Revision: I've got a ... It's ...	Pets General revision	Identifying with another culture Playing an oral game to practise vocabulary
10	I've / She's / He's got (a) (small) ... head, eyes, ears, nose, mouth, hair	Face Revision: Adjectives	Identifying and naming parts of the face Using adjectives to describe people's appearances
11	He's / She's got ... T-shirt, jumper, skirt, shoes, socks, trousers	Clothes Revision: Colours	Identifying and naming clothes Describing clothes that others are wearing Using colours as adjectives to describe clothes
12	Where's the ...? (It's) in/on the ... bed, table, chair, sofa, bed, box	Objects in the home	Identifying and naming objects in the home Asking where something is in the home Using prepositions to identify the location of an object
Project time! **Revision time!** The United Kingdom	I'm from ... My home is in ... England, Ireland, Scotland, Wales	Countries in the UK Revision	Learning about the geography of the UK Playing an oral game to practise vocabulary
Festivals Halloween			Learning how Halloween is celebrated in Britain
Festivals Christmas			Learning how Christmas is celebrated in Britain
Festivals Easter			Learning how Easter is celebrated in Britain

Introduction

General description of the course

New Chatterbox is a three-level course for children of primary school age who are learning English for the first time. There are twelve units in the Starter level and fifteen units in levels 1 and 2. A Starter level unit contains materials for three lessons of 45 minutes each with additional material for extra work in class and for homework. The Teacher's Resource Pack also provides material for one extra lesson per unit.

The components at each level are:
Starter – a Pupil's Book, an Activity Book, a Teacher's Book, a CD or cassette and a Resource Pack containing 2 posters, 80 flashcards and a Photocopy Masters book.
Levels 1 and 2 – a Pupil's Book, an Activity Book, a Teacher's Book, a CD or cassette and a combined Resource Pack containing 2 posters, 96 flashcards and a Photocopy Masters Book.

For Starter level...
The Pupil's Book presents new words, grammar structures and functions in imaginative and clear contexts. Integrated activities reinforce the new language in a fun and accessible way.
An adventure story, featuring ace detective, Captain Shadow, and a variety of songs, rhymes and games are also used to practise new language.
The Activity Book is optional and consolidates further the language points of the Pupil's Book and can be used in class or for homework. It has follow-up activities for all the Pupil's Book lessons and festival pages.
The Teacher's Book gives step-by-step lesson plans and answers, and extra ideas for classroom activities. At the end of the Teacher's Book there are ideas for adjusting lessons for different ability levels, a bank of extra games, an assessment section including four tests and a portfolio of self-assessment activities.
The Teacher's Resource Pack contains a Photocopy Masters Book with a photocopiable worksheet and an extra activity for each unit, a play, 80 flashcards and a poster. Teaching notes for the activities, posters and play are provided in the Photocopy Masters Book.

New Chatterbox Starter level – features

- An episode of the exciting Captain Shadow story in every unit.
- Projects based around cultural material.
  There is one project page every three units. Children look at British children in different parts of their lives and are encouraged to make cultural comparisons to increase cultural awareness. Children then do a project based on these comparisons.
- Fun songs and raps which revise structures and vocabulary in an interesting way.
- Fun revision games every three units.
  These provide an extra opportunity for pupils to practise and consolidate the new language learned in the previous three units.
- Festival pages for Halloween, Christmas and Easter.
  These use photos, craft activities, chants and songs to give pupils an insight into how these festivals are celebrated in Britain and provide an opportunity for cultural comparisons as well as creative work.
- A class play featuring Zak, Zeeky and the three children (Sam, Anna and Suzy), which can be found in the Photocopy Master's Book. It can be acted out in class, or used with the Oxford Puppet Theatre.

Together these features enable *New Chatterbox* to offer a package that provides a comprehensive introduction to English, which makes the learning experience more enjoyable and allows teachers to face different teaching situations with confidence.

Aims and syllabus

The main aims of *New Chatterbox Starter level* are:
- To provide young children with an enjoyable and encouraging first exposure to English through activities which are fun and relevant to their cognitive stage (e.g. songs, rhymes, games, puzzles, TPR (Total Physical Response) activities, craft activities and listening to and acting out an exciting story).
- To give them the basic tools to build up their confidence in understanding and using English.
- To develop a positive approach to learning English.

The syllabus of *New Chatterbox* has been constructed to enable communication right from the start. Simple graded structures and vocabulary have been chosen according to their frequency, usefulness and simplicity. Each language item is recycled and revised regularly.

Through interesting topics *New Chatterbox* systematically develops pupils' motivation and skills in listening, speaking, reading and, later, writing.

Introduction

Characters in *New Chatterbox Starter level*

The units are based around the adventures of Zak and Zeeky, two robot characters, who wander into a school one day and meet three children there called Anna, Sam, and Suzy. They cause chaos and get the children into trouble because they are so mischievous and are always looking for fun!

The story episodes introduce Captain Shadow, the detective, and her dog Pluto. They meet a little gang of characters – Chocolate Chip, Donut Joe (DJ), Zoko, Doris and Hubert who loves donuts!

The organization of *New Chatterbox Starter level*

Each unit of the Pupil's Book is six pages long. One unit provides work for a minimum of three 45-minute lessons. The structure of each lesson is as follows:

Start the lesson

This is a short warm-up activity to focus pupils' attention and revise language learned in recent lessons, which is sometimes through a familiar song or game.

Presentation (in Lessons 1 and 2)

The new language for the lesson is presented first with flashcards, real objects or actions off the page. This is generally vocabulary in Lesson 1 and structures for communicative exchanges in Lesson 2.

This language is then presented on the top half of the page, in context with Zak and Zeeky, and sometimes the three children. At this stage the language is for passive recognition only.

Practice

The bottom half of the first page of Lesson 1 and 2 of each unit concentrates on practice activities which show comprehension of the new language. This will usually involve listening and controlled speaking. From Unit 6 onwards the practice activity in Lesson 2 will involve controlled writing.

Further activities

Lesson 1

Captain Shadow story

The story exposes pupils to some familiar language and also some new language which they are not expected to produce but only understand in context.

Story performance

Acting out the story gives an opportunity for pupils to take part in and enjoy it for themselves. Certain areas of the language may be focused on and practised. Different individuals can act out the different characters, and everyone else can join in with sound effects etc.

Lesson 2

Song

The songs provide an opportunity to practise the target language in another context, sometimes combined with receptive language. The rhythm of the music helps develop pronunciation and word-stresses.

Song performance

This gives the opportunity for a team or group performance, for different pupils to sing different parts of a song, and for actions and props to be used to reinforce the meaning of the lyrics.

Lesson 3

Revision activities

The fifth page usually consists of activities which add a cognitive challenge to the language practice, such as a puzzle.

The sixth page combines the new language with language learned in previous units. This helps to reuse and reinforce pupils' repertoire of English.

The activity on the sixth page does not use listening skills and therefore, it can be assigned for homework or done quietly in class.

There is a picture dictionary set for each unit, which can be completed at the end of the unit or later.

Project time!

The *Project time!* pages which appear after every three units (after Units 3, 6, 9 and 12) include additional cultural material presented by British children, that pupils can easily identify with. On these pages, there is also a class project for pupils to do. The projects are followed by a revision game which reviews and recycles the language of the previous three units. Pupils should also complete a test and a self-assessment activity at these points before continuing to the next unit.

Basic procedures in *New Chatterbox Starter level*

New language presentation

New language is always first presented to pupils with their Pupil's Books closed, so that when they do open their books at the beginning of the unit, some of the words and their meanings are already familiar and interesting language practice can begin more quickly and easily.

New words and phrases are usually taught by showing real objects, by drawing simple pictures

Introduction

on the board, by using flashcards, or by mime and gesture. Wherever possible, it is best to use real objects to present new words.

Whenever a new word is introduced, make sure that pupils know how to pronounce it clearly. Say the new word two or three times. Pupils listen and repeat the new word, first of all together and then individually.

Story presentation

- Before presenting a new episode of the story, summarize what has happened in the story so far by discussing it with pupils in their mother tongue.
- Ask them to tell you briefly what they remember about previous episodes. A short summary of the preceding episode of the story appears in the teaching notes.
- Before listening to the new story episode, pre-teach some of the new words which pupils will need to understand what happens.
- Play the cassette/CD section for the story episode right through once while pupils listen and read the speech bubbles.
- Play the story again. Pupils listen a second time and repeat the sentences after the recording for pronunciation and reading practice.
- After listening to the story, go on to any further activities suggested in the notes.

Question and answer practice

Zak and Zeeky and Suzy, Sam and Anna give structure practice in Lesson 2 of each unit. The teaching notes give ideas on how this can be developed off the page. As a general procedure, begin by asking the questions yourself and helping pupils to reply. Then gradually get pupils to take over the questioning so that they are asking and answering each other.

Pair work

Question and answer practice leads naturally on to pair work, where pupils ask and answer questions in pairs. Go round checking pupils' pronunciation and understanding.

Treatment of skills in *New Chatterbox Starter level*

Listening

Listening skills are developed right from the beginning of *New Chatterbox Starter level*. All language is presented on the cassette or CD. The practice activities involve, for example, listening to identify the appropriate word to demonstrate comprehension of the target language. Many of the games require active listening as an integral part of the communication process.

Speaking

Once new language has been absorbed passively through the presentation activities, the pupils are required to use it actively in the subsequent practice work. The revision activities and games often involve speaking, and the craft activities also involve spoken language. Speech bubbles tinted in yellow in the Pupil's Book indicate language for the pupils to speak rather than read or write in. Speech bubbles in white indicate that pupils should write in them.

Reading

New Chatterbox Starter level has a strictly graded approach to reading so that pupils who are not familiar with the English alphabet or who have not been reading for very long in their mother tongue can cope easily. In Units 1-6, there are no activities which require pupils to read words. The words are there on the page for guidance and to familiarize the pupils with the way English words look. They are there for passive recognition only, so when activities which require reading skills are introduced from Unit 6 onwards, pupils have already had some exposure to English words.

As pupils' abilities in reading English develop, so do the reading challenges. Reading skills are gradually built up by first introducing children to single words and then putting these words into simple sentences. When doing reading activities, encourage pupils to develop the skill of guessing the meaning of words from their context or clues in the pictures, and not to worry if they do not understand every word.

Writing

There are no activities involving writing before Unit 6. After that, practice activities in Lesson 2 and sometimes Lesson 3 of each unit involve simple, controlled writing tasks, for example choosing the appropriate word to complete an answer or sentence.

Games

In games, pupils are able to practise using their English in the context of lively, meaningful speaking and listening activities in which they can participate without feeling self-conscious.

Project time! activities

These pages are intended to promote and develop cross-cultural awareness by teaching pupils about British culture. They are introduced to this by two British children who are featured in photos. The

Introduction

pupils learn about an aspect of their lives. There is usually an activity accompanying the photos, which uses simple reading skills. Teachers can do these activities if they feel that their class is capable of it.

At the bottom of the page, two British children demonstrate a project that pupils can replicate in class. In this way, the *Project Time!* pages are used to develop pupils' creative skills and their ability to co-operate and work with other members of the class.

Assessment

There are three forms of assessment in *New Chatterbox*:

My English is ...

This section is at the end of every unit and aims to encourage children to look back at the unit and think about what they learnt and assess their own progress.

Tests

The *New Chatterbox* tests at the back of this Teacher's Book provide a simple test of pupils' reading, writing and listening skills and should be used by the teacher to monitor individual progress and to guide future teaching. They are after every three units.

When setting a test ...
- Check that all pupils understand what they have to do. Go over the instructions and the example given for each section of the test.
- Use the pupils' results to determine where further teaching and practice may be necessary.

Portfolio

The Portfolio pages are after the tests at the back of the Teacher's Book. These photocopiable pages are designed to be used by pupils after every 3 units, to reflect on what they have achieved and what they can now do in English. You may need to go over the content of these pages with pupils in their mother tongue so that there is no confusion about any vocabulary.

- **Biography** – *Now I can ...* Pupils should look at this page, read the statements and decide which of the things they can now say/do in English. They then colour in the character for that statement.
- **Dossier** – Pupils should use this page to build up a record of all the work/projects they have done in English and record examples of their best work.
- **End-of-year review** – This should be used at the end of the year for pupils to look back over the whole year and reflect on what activities they enjoyed doing, what their best work was and what they still need to work on.

Lesson One

Language focus
Greetings and introductions: *Hello/Hi, I'm ...*
Meeting the course characters and the story characters

Classroom English
Sit down, Open your books, Close your eyes, Hello Goodbye

Starting the lesson

- Say *Hello* to your class. Encourage them all to say *Hello* back to you.
- Say *Hello* to a few individuals. They say *Hello* back to you.
- Say *Hello* (name) to about six pupils from different parts of the classroom. Gesture to all these named pupils to stand up. They then all say *Hello* to you and remain standing.
- Repeat the procedure until everyone is standing and has said *Hello*.
- Say *Sit down* and gesture to show the meaning.

Presentation

- Point to yourself and say *I'm* (name).
- Ask individuals to point to themselves and say *I'm* (name).

Practice (PUPIL'S BOOK p. 2)

01 Listen, point and say.

- Say *Open your books* and show page 2.
- Play the recording. Pupils listen.

  Tapescript
  Zak   Hello, I'm Zak.
  Zeeky   Hi! I'm Zeeky.
  Robocat   Miaow.

- Say *Listen, point and say*, using gestures to clarify the meaning. Play the recording again and pause after each speaker. Pupils point to the speaker each time and repeat their words (or the pet's noise!).
- Ask two pupils to come to the front and perform as Zak and Zeeky. If they are confident, they can do this without listening to the recording at the same time. However, they may need to speak the lines with the recording playing for support.
- Repeat the procedure with other pairs of pupils.

02 Listen and point.

- Play the recording. The pupils listen carefully and respond by pointing to the speaker each time.

  Tapescript
  Zeeky   Hi, I'm Zeeky.
  Robocat   Miaow.
  Zak   Hello, I'm Zak.

  Robocat   Miaow.
  Zak   Hello, I'm Zak.
  Zeeky   Hi, I'm Zeeky.

Quick game

- Say *Close your eyes*. Demonstrate the meaning.
- Explain that when everyone has their eyes closed, one person will be tapped on the head. This pupil should say *Hello!* or *Hi!*
- The rest of the class can then open their eyes. They have to guess who the speaker was and give their name.
- Repeat the procedure involving as many pupils as possible.

03 Story (PUPIL'S BOOK p. 3)

- Say *Open your books* and show page 3.
- Explain that the class is going to hear the first part of a story which will continue throughout the course.
- Point to each of the characters and say their names: *Pluto, Chocolate Chip* and *Donut Joe*. The pupils repeat. Explain that donuts, which feature regularly throughout the story, are deep-fried rings or balls of sweetened light dough, sometimes just sugared on top, sometimes iced with flavoured icing, and sometimes filled with jam. Chocolate Chip is not usually a name as it refers to little pieces of chocolate.
- Play the recording. Pupils listen and follow in their books.

  Tapescript
  Pluto   Look! A donut!
  Pluto   Woof!
  Donut Joe   Yes, I'm Donut Joe, the donut man.
  Chocolate Chip   Hello. DJ!
  Donut Joe   Hi, Chocolate Chip!

- Explain that the characters live near a famous canal in London, Regent's canal. It was built 200 years ago for transportation. DJ uses his boat to transport donuts from his factory to a popular nearby market.
- Play the episode right through again. Stop the tape after each line and pupils repeat it, first chorally and then individually.

Story performance
- Ask three pupils to come to the front. Play the recording. The three pupils act out the parts of Pluto, Donut Joe and Chocolate Chip. The rest of the class does the sound effects for the telephone.
- If time allows, ask other groups of pupils to act out the episode.

Ending the lesson
- Start chanting as follows and encourage the class to join in.
  Hello! Hello! Hi!
  Goodbye! Goodbye! Goodbye!
- Demonstrate the meaning of *Goodbye* by turning round and pretending to walk away, waving as you do so.
- Divide the class in half. One half chants the *Hello* line and the other half chants the *Goodbye* lines.
- Ask small groups to chant and to walk towards the door when they say *Goodbye*.

Activity Book (Optional)
If you are using the *New Chatterbox* Activity Book, use page 3 now.

Colour.
Pupils colour in the outlines of Zak, Zeeky, Anna, Sam and Suzy and then say the sentences in the speech bubbles.

Lesson 2

Language focus
Actions: *Stand up, Sit down, Open your book, Close your book, Listen, Look*
Responding to classroom instructions

Materials needed
Flashcards: *Stand up, Sit down, Open your book, Close your book, Listen, Look*

Starting the lesson
- Start chanting *Hello! Hello! Hi!* (see Lesson 1). Encourage the class to join in.
- Divide the class into two groups, one group for each line. The group which chants *Goodbye!* can pretend to leave.
- Repeat the procedure, swapping the groups.

Presentation
- Say *Stand up* as you stand up. Gesture to the class to stand up. Hold up the *Stand up* flashcard.
- Continue with *Sit down, Open your book, Look, Listen* and *Close your book*. Each time hold up the relevant flashcard and demonstrate the action clearly for pupils to copy.
- Say them again, varying the order. As pupils gain confidence stop demonstrating the actions and see if they can remember them themselves.

Practice (PUPIL'S BOOK p. 4)

04 Listen and point.
- Say *Open your books* and show page 4.
- Play the recording. Pupils listen.
  Tapescript
  Sit down, Stand up, Close your book, Listen, Open your book, Look
- Say *Listen and point*. Play the recording again and pause after each action. Display the flashcards. Pupils point to the appropriate flashcard each time.

Say and do.
- Play the recording again. Pupils join in and do the relevant actions each time.
  Tapescript
  Sit down, Stand up, Close your book, Listen, Open your book, Look.
- Arrange the class in a circle. Play the recording again and go round the circle with the first pupil demonstrating *Stand up*, the next *Sit down*, the next *Close your book* etc. Meanwhile everyone else chants the words.

05 Listen and circle.
- Show the class the second activity on the page and ask individuals to name each of the actions in the pictures (*Stand up, Sit down, Close your book, Close your book, Look, Listen*).
- Play the recording. Pause after each instruction to allow pupils to circle the appropriate picture in each pair.
  Tapescript
  Sit down
  Close your book
  Listen

Song (PUPIL'S BOOK p. 5)

06 Listen and sing.
- Say *Open your books* and show page 5.
- Play the recording. Pupils listen and look at the pictures.
  Tapescript
  Hello! Hello! Hello!
  Hi! Hi! Hi!
  Sing! Sing! Sing!
  Goodbye! Goodbye! Goodbye!
  Goodbye! Goodbye! Goodbye!
- Play the song a few more times. Encourage everyone to join in and to wave and pretend to walk away as they sing *Goodbye*.

Song performance
- Divide the class into three groups. Play the recording. Each group joins in with one of the first three lines. They all sing *Goodbye* together.
- Repeat the procedure, now asking five individuals to join in with the first five *Goodbye's* and then everyone to sing the last one loudly together.
- If you feel the pupils are confident, let them sing the song without the support of the recording.

Ending the lesson
- Call out the six actions several times in a random order. The pupils carry out or mime the actions.
- After a practice run, explain to the class that the last two or three pupils to carry out each action will leave the game. You will say *Goodbye* to them and they will move to the side.
- Play the game until you have said *Goodbye* to everyone.

Activity Book (Optional)
If you are using the *New Chatterbox* Activity Book, use page 4 now.

Draw and complete the pictures.

Pupils draw the items shown in the correct places in the pictures. If the items are too hard for pupils to copy, photocopy the page and get them to cut out the pictures and stick them in the correct places instead.

Lesson 3

Language focus
Unit 1 revision
Practising and consolidating the language.

Classroom English
Match, Let's work in pairs, Draw, OK, Good, Very good

Materials needed
Felt tip pens or crayons

Starting the lesson
- Say *Hello* to your class. Encourage them all to say *Hello* back to you.
- Say *Hello* (name) plus an action, e.g. *Open your book* or *Stand up*. The named pupil says *Hello* and does the action.
- Repeat the procedure involving as many pupils as possible. If your class is large, name more than one pupil at once to ensure that everyone has a turn.

Practice (PUPIL'S BOOK pp. 6–7)

07 Listen and match.

- Say *Open your books* and show page 6.
- Point to Zak and Zeeky and elicit their names from the pupils.
- Point to each of the action pictures and elicit the words from the pupils.
- Say *Stand up, Zak* and demonstrate drawing a line from the *Stand up* picture to the picture of Zak.
- Say *Listen and match*. Demonstrate that *Match* means to draw a joining line.
- Play the recording. Pupils listen.
- Play the recording again. Pupils draw a line from the appropriate action picture to the named character each time.

Tapescript
Stand up, Zeeky.
Look, Zeeky.
Sit down, Zak.
Close your book, Zak.
Open your book, Zeeky.
Listen, Zak.

- When everyone is ready check the activity together. Ask a pupil to give an action plus the appropriate name, e.g. *Look, Zeeky*. Check everyone agrees and look at as many books as you can to check that pupils have drawn the lines correctly.
- Continue until each line has been checked. Look at as many different books as possible.

Look and say.

- Say *Look and say* and point to the next activity.
- Say *Stand up* and demonstrate tracing along the line with your finger from the *Stand up* picture to the picture of Zeeky. Then say *Stand up, Zeeky*.
- Ask five individuals to copy your example with the other actions.
- Say *Let's work in pairs* and demonstrate the meaning of this. Pupils take turns saying an action and tracing along the line to find the character and say their name.

Look and say.

- Say *Look and say* and point to the next activity on page 7.
- Start reading Zeeky's speech bubble. Encourage the class to say Zeeky's sentence, saying *I'm Zeeky*.

Draw and say.

- Indicate the empty frame and say *Draw*. Demonstrate drawing a (very simple!) self-portrait on the board. When you have finished, point to the picture and say *I'm* (name).
- Encourage the pupils to do the same. Go round helping and listening to them saying *I'm* (name).

My English is ...

- Hold up your book, indicating Unit 1 and ask the class, *Is Unit 1 OK, Good or Very good?*
- Say *OK* and show the meaning with your facial expression. Repeat the procedure with *Good* and *Very Good*.
- Show the class the *My English is ...* section in their books. Explain to the class that they should think about the unit and what they have learnt and how confident they feel about it. If they are not very confident, they should tick *OK*. If they are quite confident but don't remember everything, they should tick *Good*, and if they feel very confident and can remember everything, they should tick *Very Good*.
- Encourage them to tick the box which reflects their feelings about the unit. Check if anyone has ticked *OK* and make time later to establish whether there was anything they did not understand.

Revision game

- Say *Pluto says Stand up*. Everyone stands.
- Explain that they must follow your instructions only if you say *Pluto says*. If you do not say *Pluto says*, they continue with the action they were doing before.

Ending the lesson

- Sing the *Hello! Goodbye!* song with the recording from Lesson 2.
- Divide the class into four groups, one group for each line of the song.
- When it is time to finish, the group singing *Goodbye* move to the door.
- Divide the remaining children into four groups again. Again, the group who sings *Goodbye* moves to the door.
- Continue until everyone is at the door, then say *Goodbye* to everyone again.

Activity Book (Optional)

If you are using the *New Chatterbox* Activity Book, use page 5 now.

Read and colour.

Pupils read the words and colour in the pictures, so they associate the picture and the command.

Unit 1 Extra activities

Action circle

Language practised
Stand up, Sit down, Look, Listen, Open your book, Close your book

- Arrange the class in a circle. Encourage one pupil to give an instruction to the pupil on their left. This pupil does the action and then gives a different instruction to the pupil on their left.
- This continues around the circle until everyone has had a turn. If the class can cope, ask the first child to start another chain of actions shortly after the first one, so that everyone has to keep concentrating.

Soft ball

Language practised
Hello, Hi, I'm (name), *Goodbye*

Materials
A soft ball

- Arrange the class in a circle. Throw or pass a soft ball to a pupil and encourage them to say *Hello* or *Hi, I'm* (name). They then pass or throw the ball either to the next pupil or across the circle to a different pupil, and so on.
- A pupil who has just received the ball can choose to say *Goodbye*. Everyone must then turn away from the circle and wave their hands. You then start the game again by throwing the ball to a new pupil.

Lesson 1

Language focus
Numbers: *1–10*
Recognising and identifying numbers in English, equating numbers with amounts

Classroom English
Draw, I'm ready

Materials needed
Flashcards: *1–10*

Starting the lesson

- Say *Hello* to your class. Encourage them all to say *Hello* back to you.
- Encourage everyone to say *Hello* or *Hi, I'm (name)* to their neighbour.
- Give instructions to the whole class, e.g. *Stand up, Open your book, Look* etc. The class carries out or mimes the actions.
- Ask a pupil to give an instruction to another pupil, e.g. *Open your book,* (name). The named pupil does the action then gives a different instruction to another pupil.
- Sing the *Hello! Goodbye song!* from Unit 1 Lesson 2.

Presentation

- Start counting *1–10* on your fingers. Some pupils may be able to join in.
- Position the number flashcards in consecutive order around the room. Count slowly and point to each number as you say it. The class copies you. As they gain confidence, start to count more quickly.
- Continue counting but stop pointing. Encourage pupils to point.
- Divide the class in half and ask one half to *Stand up*. Encourage the other half to count while the pupils who are standing up point to the flashcards. Swap the groups and repeat the procedure.

Practice (PUPIL'S BOOK p. 8)

(08) Listen, point and say.

- Say *Open your books* and show page 8. Point to the characters and elicit *Zak* and *Zeeky* from the class.
- Play the recording. Pupils listen.
Tapescript
Zak and Zeeky   1 2 3 4 5 6 7 8 9 10

- Say *Listen, point and say*. Play the recording again and pause after each number. Pupils point to the appropriate block each time and repeat the number.
- Say *Let's work in pairs*. Play the recording again. Pupils take turns in their pair or small groups pointing and saying the numbers with Zak and Zeeky.

(09) Listen and draw.

- Make sure the number flashcards are still visible. Say a number and ask individuals to point to the appropriate card.
- Say a number, e.g. *7*, and ask a pupil to point to the right flashcard. Then, ask another pupil to come to the front and draw seven squares on the board. Repeat this procedure several times.
- Show pupils the *Listen and draw* activity in their books. Explain that you will play the recording and they should draw the right number of boxes in each frame.
- Play the recording. Pause after each number. Play it again for pupils to check their work. Go round helping where necessary.
Tapescript and Answers
9 3 6 1 7 5
- When everyone is ready, check the activity together. Play the recording and after each number ask a pupil to come and draw the right numbers of squares on the board.

(10) Story (PUPIL'S BOOK p. 9)

- Say *Open your books* and show page 9.
- Ask if the class can remember what happened in the first episode of the story, in Unit 1: Pluto, followed the delicious smell of donuts onto the canal boat of Donut Joe, but Donut Joe doesn't know that Pluto is on the boat.
- Play the recording. Pupils follow in their books.
Tapescript

Donut Joe	OK, Chocolate Chip. Yes, I'm ready now.
Donut Joe	1 – 2, 1 – 2 – 3 … Donuts for you and me! 4 – 5, 4- 5 – 6.
Pluto	Oh no!
Chocolate Chip	Hi, Donut Joe!
Donut Joe	Hello, Chocolate Chip!

- Ask pupils to count the donuts in the different pictures.
- Play the recording again. Encourage the class to join in with the counting of the donuts.
- See if anyone can guess what *I'm ready* means. Encourage pupils to use it at appropriate moments.

Story performance
- Ask three pupils to come to the front. Play the recording again. The three pupils act out the parts of Pluto, Donut Joe and Chocolate Chip. The rest of the class joins in counting the donuts.
- If time allows, ask other groups of pupils to act out the episode.

Ending the lesson
- Count round the class with each pupil saying a number. Each time a pupil says *10*, that pupil says *Goodbye* and stands to the side or moves to the door.
- Continue until everyone has said *Goodbye*.

Activity Book (Optional)
If you are using the *New Chatterbox* Activity Book use page 6 now.

Count and match.
Pupils count the number of each item and draw a line to the correct number.

Lesson 2

Language focus
What's this? It's a …, bag, rubber, pen, pencil, book, pencil case

Function
Identifying classroom objects, asking and answering simple questions

Materials needed
A large piece of cloth, a smaller school bag, a rubber, a pen, a pencil, a book, a pencil case
Flashcards: *1–10*

Starting the lesson
- Say *Hello* to the class. They reply.
- Say *Stand up*. Start counting from 1–10. When you reach *10* elicit a big HELLO from the class.
- Ask a group of pupils to count 1–10. When they reach *10* everyone shouts HELLO.
- Repeat the procedure involving as many pupils as possible in the counting. Then ask everyone to *Sit down*.

Presentation
- Hold up each of the classroom objects and say the word for the class to repeat.
- Secretly wrap one of the objects in a piece of cloth. Ask pupils to feel the object through the cloth. Ask *What's this?* Elicit an answer (e.g. *book*) and repeat the answer saying *It's a book*.
- Repeat this procedure, changing the objects, allowing as many pupils as possible to guess what they are.

Practice (PUPIL'S BOOK p. 10)

11 Listen and point.
- Say *Open your books* and show page 10.
- Point to the bag Anna is holding and say *What's this?* See if anyone can answer *It's a bag*.
- Play the recording. Pupils listen.

Tapescript
Zeeky	What's this?
Anna	It's a bag. What's this?
Sam	It's a rubber. What's this?
Zak	It's a pencil. What's this?
Suzy	It's a book. What's this?
Robocat	It's a pen. What's this?
Zeeky	It's a pencil case.

- Say *Listen and point*. Play the recording again and pause after each classroom object. Pupils point to the right object each time.

Play and say.
- Ask six pupils to come to the front. Give each of them a classroom object: bag, rubber, pen, book, pencil, pencil case.
- Play the recording. Pupils hold up their objects when they hear them. The rest of the class points at the right object.
- Ask six different pupils to come to the front. Repeat the procedure but this time each pupil holds up their object and asks the next pupil *What's this?*
- The next pupil answers, e.g. *It's a pen* and takes the object. They then hold up their original object and ask the next pupil *What's this?* and so on.
- Continue, asking different groups of pupils to come to the front.

Draw and say.
- Show the class the second activity. Demonstrate tracing over the dots to complete the pencil and ask a pupil *What's this?* They answer *It's a pencil*.
- Ask pupils to trace each object. Go round asking individuals *What's this?* as they work.
- When they are ready, say *Let's work in pairs*. One pupil in each pair or small group points to a completed object and asks *What's this?* The other pupil answers *It's a …* . They swap roles and continue.
- Go round listening and helping.

🔊 Song (PUPIL'S BOOK p. 11)
- Say *Open your books.* Show them page 11.
- Play the recording of the *Number Samba* song. Pupils listen and look at the pictures.

   Tapescript
   1, 2 …
   1, 2, 3 …
   1, 2, 3, 4, 5 …
   6, 7 …
   6, 7, 8 …
   6, 7, 8, 9, 10!

- Play the song a few more times. Encourage everyone to join in and to clap to the beat.
- Hand out the number flashcards. Play the song again and ask everyone with a card to hold it up at the right moment in the song.

Song performance
- Divide the class into two groups. Play the recording again. Each group joins in with one of the verses. They all clap to the rhythm and dance.
- Ask small groups to sing the song and to dance. Everyone else claps to the rhythm.

Ending the lesson
- Call out the six classroom objects. Each time the pupils mime using that object (pen and pencil will be the same).
- After practising this once or twice, explain to the class that the last two or three pupils to mime using each object will leave the game. You will say *Goodbye* to them and they will move to the side.
- Play the game until you have said *Goodbye* to everyone.

Activity Book (Optional)
If you are using the *New Chatterbox* Activity Book, use page 7 now.

Match and draw.
Pupils draw a line from each character to the object which belongs to them and then draw the object in the correct place. Draw attention to the collar as it is very important in the story. (The collar contains a tracking device which enables his owner to find him.)

Circle 5 differences.
Pupils look at the two pictures and circle the five differences between them.

Lesson 3

Language focus
Unit 2 revision.

Function
Practising and consolidating the language.

Classroom English
Let's count the … (Note: pupils will hear the plural *s* but will not be expected to use it actively)

Materials needed
A bag, a rubber, a pen, a pencil, a book, a pencil case

Starting the lesson
- Greet the class as usual. Start counting from *1–10* and encourage the class to join in.
- Pupils continue counting *1–10* around the class. Each time they reach *10* hold up one of the classroom objects and ask *What's this?* Ask individuals or the whole class to reply *It's a … .*

Practice (PUPIL'S BOOK pp. 12–13)
Look, count and write.
- Say *Open your books* and show page 12.
- Point to a few of the items in the picture and ask *What's this?*
- Say *Let's count the pencils.* Do this as a class and demonstrate writing the number 6 into the box by the picture of the pencils.
- Pupils continue with the activity by themselves.
- When everyone is ready, check the activity together. Say, e.g. *Let's count the rubbers* and ask a pupil to count. Check everyone agrees.

Colour 5 numbers.

🔊 Listen and play.
Tapescript
5, 7, 2, 9, 1, 8, 3, 4, 10, 6

- Prepare for the next activity by writing numbers *1–10* on the board but in a random order. Ask individuals to come and circle the numbers as you say them.
- Write isolated numbers on the board and ask pupils to call them out
- Point to the rubric *Colour 5 numbers.* Ask everyone to choose five numbers to colour.
- When everyone is ready say *Listen and play.* Play the recording. Pupils circle the numbers they have coloured when they hear them. They do not circle the ones they have not coloured.
- The first pupil to circle five coloured numbers is the winner, but the game can continue until everyone has circled five coloured numbers.

- The game can be played again if pupils colour in all the numbers and then pick five on which they place a counter (or a small piece of paper). Choose a pupil to call out numbers *1–10* at random. Each time the pupils hear one of their chosen numbers they remove the relevant counter. The first pupil to remove all five counters puts up their hand.

Ask and answer.

- Hold up page 13. Explain that Zak, Zeeky and Robocat are each holding two fishing lines which they are trying to hook onto the objects in the pool.
- Point out the objects in the pool and ask individuals *What's this?*
- Say *Let's work in pairs*. The pupils in each pair take turns to be Zak, Zeeky and Robocat, asking and answering questions about the objects at the end of their fishing lines. Go round listening and helping.

My English is …

Follow the procedure that is outlined on page 11.

Ending the lesson

- Sing the *Number Samba* song from Lesson 2. Ask small groups to take turns performing the song.
- Say *Goodbye* to the class.

Activity Book (Optional)

If you are using the *New Chatterbox* Activity Book, use page 8 now.

Find and circle.

Pupils read the word, look at the picture, and find and circle this word in the line.

Draw, colour and say.

Pupils join up the dots, colour in the completed pictures and say the words.

Unit 2 Extra activities

Circle game

Language practised
What's this? It's a … bag, pen, pencil case, book, rubber, pencil

Materials
a bag, a pen, a pencil case, a book, a rubber, a pencil

- Arrange the class in a circle. Give a classroom item, e.g. a pencil, to a pupil. They offer it to the next pupil asking *What's this?* The next pupil takes the pencil saying *It's a pencil.*
- This continues around the circle until everyone has had a turn. If the class can cope, give the first pupil another object to pass round shortly after the first one, so that everyone has to keep concentrating.

1-2-3 Stand up

Language practised
Numbers 1–10, *Stand up, Sit down, Look, Listen, Open your book, Close your book*

- Ask a pupil to say a number (e.g. 7). Then ask a different pupil to say an instruction (e.g. *Open your book*).
- The whole class counts to the number and then does the action, e.g. they all count *1–7* and then all open their books.
- Continue the procedure with different pupils choosing the numbers and the instructions.

Soft ball

Language practised
Numbers 1–10

Materials
A soft ball

- Arrange the class in a circle. Call *1* as you throw a soft ball to a pupil. They then call *2* as they throw to another pupil and so on.
- Continue until they get to *10*. Then start again at *1*, throwing the ball to a pupil who has not yet had a turn.

Lesson 1

Language focus
Family: *mum, dad, sister, brother*
Introducing members of the family: *This is my ...*

Materials needed
Flashcards: *1–4, mum, dad, sister, brother*

Starting the lesson

- Say *Hello* to your class. Encourage them all to say *Hello* back to you.
- Encourage everyone to say *Hello* or *Hi, I'm (name)* to their neighbour.
- Start counting and encourage pupils to continue counting around the class. Start again when they reach 10.
- Sing the *Number Samba* song from Unit 2, Lesson 2.

Presentation

- Ask four pupils to come to the front and give them each a family flashcard (*mum, dad, brother* or *sister*).
- Go to each of them and introduce them, saying, e.g. *This is my dad*. Do this a few times so that the class becomes familiar with the family words.
- Go to each family member again and say *This is my ...* . Pause to allow the class to supply the family word.

Practice (PUPIL'S BOOK p. 14)

14 Listen, point and say.

- Say *Open your books* and show page 14. Point to Zak and elicit *Zak* from the class.
- Play the recording. Pupils listen.
  Tapescript
  This is my mum.
  This is my dad.
  This is my sister.
  This is my brother.
- Say *Listen, point and say*. Play the recording again and pause after each line. Display the flashcards for *mum, dad, sister* and *brother*. Pupils point to the family member flashcard each time and repeat the line.
- Say *Let's work in pairs*. Play the recording again. Pupils take turns in their pair or small groups pointing and repeating the sentence at the same time.

15 Listen and number.

- Ask four different pupils to come the front and give them each a flashcard for the four family members. Have ready four number flashcards (1–4) and ask four more pupils to come to the front and each hold up one of the cards.
- Say, e.g. *3. My sister*. The pupil with the number 3 flashcard comes and stands next to the pupil with the *sister* flashcard.
- Continue with different numbers and different family members.
- Show pupils the *Listen and number* activity in their books. Explain that you will play the recording and they should write the right number in the box next to each family member picture.
- Play the recording. Pause after each line. Play it again for pupils to check their work. Go round helping where necessary.
  Tapescript
  1. My sister.
  2. My mum.
  3. My dad.
  4. My brother.
- When everyone is ready check the activity together. Check any misunderstandings.

16 Story (PUPIL'S BOOK p. 15)

- Say *Open your books* and show page 15.
- Ask if the class can remember what happened in the second episode of the story, in Unit 2: Pluto is still in the boat, hidden under a table which is covered in delicious donuts. Donut Joe has set off to market with another tray of donuts, locking the door of the boat behind him.
- Play the recording. The pupils follow in their books.
  Tapescript
  Pluto   Ooowww!
  Captain Shadow Pluto? Pluto?
  Captain Shadow Good! It's Pluto – listen!
                         BLEEP – BLEEP
  Captain Shadow Look! He's at the market!
  Luke   Well done, Captain!
  Captain Shadow OK – let's go!
- Check that the pupils understand that Captain Shadow can pick up Pluto's tracker on her computer, Luke.
- Play the episode right through again. Stop the tape after each line and pupils repeat it, first chorally and then individually.

Story performance
- Ask two pupils to come to the front. Play the recording. The two pupils act out the parts of Captain Shadow and Luke. The rest of the class does the sound effects for Pluto howling and for the tracker device in Pluto's name tag.
- If time allows, ask other pairs to act out the episode.

Ending the lesson
- Ask everyone to choose whether they are mums, dad, brothers or sisters. Give instructions for the family members to carry out, e.g. S*tand up, mums; Open your books, sisters* etc.
- Say, e.g. *Goodbye, brothers*. All the brothers say *Goodbye* and move to the door. Continue until you have said *Goodbye* to everyone.

(Note: Ask each pupil to bring a photo of their mum, dad, brother or sister to the next lesson.)

Activity Book (Optional)
If you are using the *New Chatterbox* Activity Book, use page 9 now.

Look and number.
Pupils look at the picture and write the number of each family member in the box below, next to the pictures and labels.

Write.
Pupils trace the words and colour in the pictures.

Lesson 2

Language focus
Who's this? This is my ...
Asking and answering about family members
happy, sad

Materials needed
Photos of a typical mum, dad, brother and sister, glue
Each pupil needs to bring in a photo of one family member: their mum, dad, brother or sister
Flashcards: *happy, sad*

Starting the lesson
- Say *Hello* to the class. They reply.
- Divide the class into four groups, one group for *mum*, one for *dad*, one for *brother* and one for *sister*.
- Hold up your photos saying, e.g. *This is my brothe*r. All the pupils in the *brother* group stand up.
- Repeat the procedure, moving quickly from one family member to another so that the pupils have to concentrate and listen carefully.

Presentation
- Hold up one of your photos, look puzzled and ask *Who's this?* Encourage the class to repeat the question a few times. Give the answer, e.g. *My dad*.
- Hold up the other photos and each time elicit the question *Who's this?*
- Ask four pupils to come to the front. They each hold up one of your photos and ask *Who's this?* You answer them.

Practice (PUPIL'S BOOK p. 16)
Ask and answer.
- Say *Open your books* and show page 16. Say *Ask and answer*.
- Ask one pupil to be Zak. They hold up the book and point to each of the photos, each time asking *Who's this?* The rest of the class takes the part of Suzy and answers, e.g. *my sister*.
- Say *Let's work in pairs*. In each pair one pupil takes the part of Suzy and the other takes the part of Zak. Zak points to each photo asking *Who's this?* and Suzy answers.
- Go round listening and helping.

Draw and say.
- Hold up your photos and say, e.g. *This is my brother*.
- Demonstrate copying the person in the photo by drawing the person into the empty frame on the Pupil's Book page and encourage the pupils to do the same.
- Hold up your book with the picture and say, e.g. *This is my mum*. Encourage as many pupils as possible to do the same. If there is not much time, encourage them to show their photos to their neighbours instead of to the class and say, e.g. *This is my dad*.

🔊 Song (PUPIL'S BOOK p. 17)
- Say *Open your books* and show page 17.
- Play the recording. The pupils listen and look at the pictures.

Tapescript
This is my mum, mum, mum
This is my dad, dad, dad.
My mum is always happy,
And my dad is never sad!

This is my brother, brother.
This is my sister, sister.
My brother is always happy.
And my sister is never sad!

- Hold up the *happy* and *sad* flashcards and say the words. The class repeats. Hold up the flashcards and encourage the class to say the words. Put down the flashcards. Say *happy* and *sad* and encourage the class to make the right facial expressions.
- Play the recording again. Encourage the class to make happy and sad expressions when they hear the words. If they ask, explain to them the meaning of *never* and *always*.

Song performance
- Divide the class into two groups. One group sings the 'always happy' lines (*My mum is/ brother is always happy*) and the other group sings the 'never sad' (*My dad is/sister is never sad*) lines. Everyone sings the other lines. Encourage plenty of mime and gesture.

Ending the lesson
- Arrange the class into groups of two. Each group decides who is the mum and who is the dad.
- Say *Goodbye, Mum* and then *Goodbye, Dad*.
- When they are called, they move towards the door.

(Note: Ask each pupil to keep their photos for use in the next lesson.)

Activity Book (Optional)
If you are using the *New Chatterbox* Activity Book use page 10 now.

Draw and complete the pictures.
Pupils look at the story episode. There are items missing from the pictures. Pupils draw the missing items back into the pictures. They can look back at the story episode in the Pupil's Book if they need to. If the pictures are too hard for pupils to copy, photocopy the page for them and they can cut out the pictures and stick them in the correct places.

Lesson 3

Language focus
Unit 3 revision

Function
Practising and consolidating the language

Classroom English
Let's count the ... (Note: pupils will hear the plural *s* but will not be expected to use it actively)

Materials needed
Each pupil needs their photos of family members from the last lesson

Three counters for each group of two or three pupils
Flashcards: *mum, dad, sister, brother, pen, pencil, pencil case, rubber, book, bag*

Starting the lesson
- Greet the class as usual. Hold up the family photos and elicit *Who's this?* from the class. Answer, e.g. *my sister*.
- Ask individuals to bring their family photos to the front and show them to the class. They introduce them, saying, e.g. *This is my mum, this is my sister* etc.

Practice (PUPIL'S BOOK pp. 18–19)
Play and say.
- Say *Open your books* and show page 18.
- Point to a few of the items in the picture and ask *What's this?*
- Point to a couple of the family members and say *This is my* ... . Pause for the class to supply the right word.
- Hide one counter in one of your hands and two counters in the other. Ask a pupil to come to the front and choose one of your hands. They take the counter or counters and say *1* or *2*.
- Now demonstrate moving the same number of sections on the game. If the pupil has chosen one counter, move to section 1, point to the pencil and ask *What's this?* The pupil answers *It's a pencil*. If the pupil has chosen two counters, move to section 2, point to the picture of Zak's mum and encourage the pupil to pretend to be Zak and say *This is my mum*.
- Arrange the class into pairs or small groups and give each pair or small group three counters.
- Say *Let's play*. Everyone starts to play as you have demonstrated. Move round the class listening and helping. If some pairs finish before others, suggest they form new pairs and play again.

Draw your family and say.
- Show the class the picture of Zeeky and her family on page 19.
- Ask them to stick in their family photo or draw a picture of their family in the empty frame provided.
- Go around helping them to say the words in the speech bubble and to introduce their family, e.g. *I'm* (name). *This is my sister, this is my mum, this is my brother*.
- Ask each pupil to introduce their family to their neighbour.

My English is ...
Follow the procedure that is outlined on page 11.

Picture game (revision).
- Have ready flashcards for *mum, dad, sister, brother, pen, pencil, pencil case, rubber, book* and *bag*.
- Arrange the pupils in a circle. Hand round the flashcards, face down.
- Play some music while the pupils pass round the flashcards. When you stop the music they stop passing and the pupils with flashcards hold them up.
- Each pupil with an object flashcard asks *What's this?* The class answers *It's a ...* .
- Each pupil with a family member flashcard asks *Who's this?* The class answers, e.g. *dad*.
- Continue the procedure so that as many pupils as possible have a turn.

Ending the lesson
- Say *I'm happy* and make a happy face. Encourage the class to copy you.
- Say *I'm sad* and make a sad face. Encourage the class to copy you.
- Sing the *Mum, mum, mum ... Dad, dad, dad* song from Lesson 2. Hand out the *Mum, Dad, brother* and *sister* flashcards for pupils to hold up at the relevant moments.
- Say *Goodbye* to the class.

Activity Book (Optional)
If you are using the *New Chatterbox* Activity Book, use page 11 now.

Find and match.
Pupils look at the big picture. They then look at the little pictures below and match the beginning of the sentences with the correct ends.

Unit 3 Extra activities

Family circle game
Language practised
This is my ... sister, brother, mum, dad.

- Arrange the class in a circle. Explain that they are all going to pretend that the pupil next to them is a member of their family.
- Introduce the pupil next to you to the rest of the class saying, e.g. *This is my mum*. This will create some amusement.
- Continues around the circle with everyone introducing their neighbour.

Draw a family tree
Language practised
Family members (If the pupils can cope you can introduce *granny, grandad, aunt, uncle*.)

- Draw a family tree on the board, with simple pictures of a mum and dad on one level and children on the level below them. If you wish you can add grandparents and uncles and aunts. Write simple text labels, e.g. *mum, dad, brother* etc.
- Pupils draw their own family trees. They do not need to write the text labels.
- Go round admiring and asking *Who's this?*

 (PUPIL'S BOOK p. 20)

Extra language
Find my ... classroom, family. This is me.

Materials needed
A sheet of paper for each pupil, scissors, glue or sticky tape, a large backing sheet, dice for each pair of pupils, a counter for each pupil
Display board: Cover a large area of wall (perhaps 1x2 meters) with coloured paper to make a display board.

18 Listen and match.

- Say *Open your books*. Show page 20. Allow the pupils time to look at the photos.
- Play the recording. It is unlikely at this stage that the class will be able to follow all the words in their books, but they will recognize familiar words which will help them identify which photo is being referred to.

Tapescript
Ben Hi! I'm Ben.
This is my family. Find my mum, my dad, my brother, my sister and me!
This is my classroom. Find a book, a bag, and a pencil case!

- Read the first sentence of each speech bubble again. Ask the class to point at the corresponding photo. Read the other sentences and allow time for the class to point at the right photos.

Find.

- Ask pupils to find the named objects in the photos. Check that everyone has found them by holding up your book and asking pupils to come up and point to them individually.

Make a class picture.

- Draw attention to the class picture at the bottom of page 20. Explain that they are going to make a similar picture.
- Hand out a sheet of paper to each pupil and ask them to draw a picture of themselves. Make sure you do one of yourself too! When they are ready, ask them to hold up their pictures and say *This is me*. Practise this a few times, first as a class and then individually.
- Have ready a large sheet of backing paper. Ask the class slowly and carefully to arrange their pictures onto the backing sheet.

- Stick the class picture onto the display board. Encourage the class to show it to their parents and friends and teachers from other classes. They can point to themselves and others, saying e.g. *This is me, this is* (name) etc.

End the lesson

- Gather the pupils round the display board. Ask individuals to point to the photos and say, e.g. *This is my friend, this is me*, etc.
- Say *Goodbye* to the whole class.

Activity Book (Optional)
If you are using the *New Chatterbox* Activity Book, use page 12 now.

Look and ✓ or ✗.
Pupils look at the two pictures. Then they look at the list of items below each picture and tick the box if the item is in the picture and cross the box if it is not.

Draw and ✓ or ✗.
Pupils draw their own bags with items of their choice inside. Then they look at the list of items and tick the box if they have drawn the item and cross the box if they have not.

Revision time! (PUPIL'S BOOK p. 21)

- Say *Open your books* and show page 21. Ask individuals to name the items in the circles on the page.
- Make sure everyone knows where to find the stickers for the game – in the insert in the middle of the book.
- Arrange the class into pairs or small groups. Explain how to play the game.
  1 Start at the start sign and throw a dice.
  2 Count round the course according to the number you throw.
  3 Name the item or action in the picture you land on. If you say the word correctly (your partner or other group members or your teacher will say if it is correct) find the corresponding sticker and stick it on.
  4 Take turns to throw until you have landed on all the circles and have covered them all with stickers. Once you have been round once, carry on round again and again.

Test
Ask pupils to do Test 1.

Unit 4

Lesson 1

Language focus
Colours: *white, green, black, yellow, red, blue*
Recognizing the colour word and distinguishing between the colours

Materials needed
Flashcards: *white, green, black, yellow, red* and *blue*
Flashcards 1–6

Starting the lesson

- Say *Hello* to your class. Encourage them all to say *Hello* back to you.
- Say *I'm happy* and make a happy face. Then say *I'm sad* and make a sad face.
- Call out individual pupils' names and encourage them to say either *I'm happy* or *I'm sad*, making the appropriate faces.
- Sing the *Mum, mum, mum* song from Unit 3, Lesson 2.

Presentation

- Have ready the flashcards for *white*, *green*, *black*, *yellow*, *red* and *blue*. Ask six pupils to stand in different places around the classroom and hold up their flashcard.
- Point to each flashcard and say the colour word. The class repeats.
- Ask the six pupils to swap places with each other. Say the colour words again and ask the class to point to the appropriate colours. Repeat this a few times.

Practice (PUPIL'S BOOK p. 22)

22 Listen, point and say.

- Say *Open your books* and show page 22.
- Play the recording. Pupils listen.
  Tapescript
  blue, red, black, white, green, yellow
- Say *Listen, point and say*. Play the recording again and pause after each colour. Pupils point to the appropriate paint tin each time and repeat the colour word.
- Say *Let's work in pairs*. Play the recording again. Pupils take turns in their pair or small groups pointing and saying the right colour word with the recording.

23 Listen and colour.

- Ask six pupils to come to the front, Give each of them a flashcard.
- Ask six different pupils to come the front. Give each of them a number card *1–6*.
- Say, e.g. *3. blue*. The pupil with the number *3* flashcard comes and stands next to the pupil with the blue flashcard.
- Continue with different numbers and different colours.
- Show pupils the *Listen and colour* activity in their books. Explain that you will play the recording and they should colour the balloon with the number they hear, in the colour they hear.
- Play the recording. Pause after each line. Play each line again for pupils to colour the right balloon. Go round helping where necessary.
  Tapescript
  1. red.
  2. white.
  3. blue.
  4. black.
  5. green.
  6. yellow.
- When everyone is ready, check the activity together. Play the recording, and after each number and colour, ask two pupils to come to the front and hold up the right number card and the correct colour flashcard. Check any misunderstandings.

24 Story (PUPIL'S BOOK p. 23)

- Say *Open your books* and show page 23.
- Ask if the class can remember what happened in the third episode of the story in Unit 3: Captain Shadow tracked Pluto by following the tracker device in his name-tag. Through her computer, Luke, she has located him, so they have set off to rescue him.
- Play the recording. Pupils follow in their books.
  Tapescript
  Luke   Wow! Great!
  Luke   Look, Captain. Pluto is in the boat!
  Chocolate Chip   Hi! I'm Chocolate Chip!
  Captain Shadow   Hello. I'm Captain Shadow. My dog is in this boat.
  Pluto   Ooowww!
  Captain Shadow   It's OK, Pluto – I'm here.
  Chocolate Chip   Well done, Pluto! Good dog! Here!
  Pluto   Woof! Woof!
- To check comprehension of the story, ask questions in the pupils' language about the story, e.g. *Why does Luke say 'Wow! Great!'?* (he likes the motorbike ride), *Why does Chocolate Chip say 'Well done!' to Pluto?*

(because Pluto manages not to eat any of the donuts).
- Play the recording again. This time encourage everyone to join in with *Well done, Pluto! Good dog!*

Story performance
- Ask three pupils to come to the front. Play the recording. The three pupils act out the parts of Captain Shadow, Luke and Chocolate Chip. The rest of the class does the sound effects for Pluto howling and for the tracker disk in his name-tag.
- If time allows, ask other groups to act out the episode.

Ending the lesson
- Explain you will say a colour. Anyone wearing anything in that colour stands up, moves to the door and says *Goodbye*.
- Continue until everyone has said *Goodbye*.

Activity Book (Optional)
If you are using the *New Chatterbox* Activity Book use page 13 now.

Colour.
Pupils look at the key and colour each letter the colour indicated to complete the banner.

Read and colour.
Pupils read the colour on the gift tag and colour the present the same colour.

Lesson 2

Language focus
How old are you? I'm ...
Asking and answering about age

Materials needed
Flashcards from Lesson 1, a badge showing 7.

Starting the lesson
- Say *Hello* to the class. They reply.
- Hold up the flashcards from Lesson 1. The pupils call out the colours.
- Divide the class into six groups, one for each colour. Say, e.g. *Stand up, red*. The pupils in the red group all stand up. Continue with, e.g. *Open your books, blue, Listen, yellow* etc.

Presentation
- Count 1–10 with the class.
- Ask a pupil to come to the front (ideally one who is 7 years old). Attach the badge to the pupil and ask *How old are you?* Help the pupil reply *I'm 7*.
- Ask several individuals *How old are you?* They reply *I'm ...* .

Practice (PUPIL'S BOOK p. 24)

Ask and answer.
- Say *Open your books* and show page 24. Say *Ask and answer*.
- Ask all the boys to read Sam's speech bubble and all the girls to answer as Suzy.
- Ask a boy and girl to come the front. The girl wears the age badge. They carry out the exchange in the book with the boy asking *How old are you?* and the girl answering *I'm 7*.
- Say *Let's work in pairs*. In each pair, pupils take turns asking and answering the question *How old are you?*
- Go round listening and helping.

25 Listen, write and say.
- Show the next activity. Explain that the pupils will listen and write the correct age on each badge.
- Play the recording. Pause after each question and answer to give pupils time to write in the age.

Tapescript
1	How old are you?
Zeeky	I'm 5.
2	How old are you?
Anna	I'm 8.
3	How old are you?
Zak	I'm 7.
4	How old are you?
Sam	I'm 8.

- Check the activity together. Play each question and answer and ask a pupil to write the number on the board.
- Say *Let's work in pairs*. Arrange the class into pairs or small groups. They take turns asking and answering *How old are you? I'm ...* for each character.
- Go round listening and helping.

26 Song (PUPIL'S BOOK p. 25)
- Say *Open your books* and show page 25.
- Explain that it is Pluto's birthday and the class is going to sing to him.
- Play the recording a couple of times, encouraging everyone to join in.

Tapescript
Happy Birthday to you!
Happy Birthday to you!
Happy Birthday, dear Pluto!
Happy Birthday to you!

- Ask if anyone in the class has a birthday soon and sing the song to them. Remember to sing the right name!

Ending the lesson
- Ask a pupil *How old are you?* Tell them not to reply but instead to jump the appropriate number of times for their age. They then say *I'm...*, pause, and wait for the class to supply the number.
- Repeat the procedure with a few pupils.
- Ask a pupil *How old are you?* They reply, e.g. *I'm 6.* Say *Stand up.* Encourage all the other 6 year olds to stand up and repeat *I'm 6.*
- Say *Goodbye* to all the 6 year olds. They reply *Goodbye* and move towards the door.
- Repeat the procedure with all the other age groups in the class.

Activity Book (Optional)
If you are using the *New Chatterbox* Activity Book, use page 14 now.

Write the number.
Pupils number the story pictures in the same order they appear in the Pupil's Book.

Colour.
Pupils look at the frame from the story episode and colour it in the right colours.

Lesson 3

Language focus
Unit 4 revision

Function
Practising and consolidating the language.

Materials needed
Flashcards: *white*, *green*, *black*, *yellow*, *red* and *blue*

Starting the lesson
- Greet the class as usual. Hold up the flashcards. The class calls the colour each time.
- Divide the class into six groups and give them each a colour.
- Call out the colours in varying order. Each group jumps up and down again when they hear their colour.

Practice (PUPIL'S BOOK pp. 26–27)

27 Listen, write and draw.

- Ask a few pupils *How old are you?* They answer *I'm ... .*
- Say *Open your books* and show page 26.
- Play the first question and answer on the recording. Pause and look at the first picture. Ask *How old are you?* and answer *I'm ... .* Pause for the class to supply the answer *10*.
- Ask a pupil to count the candles on the cake and read the number on the badge.
- Continue to play the recording. Pause after each question and answer, for the class to draw the appropriate number of candles on the cake and to write the number on the badge.
- Check the activity together. Ask individuals to answer as the children on the page when you ask them *How old are you?* Different pupils can then come to the front and draw the right number of candles on the cake and the age on the badge.

Tapescript
1 How old are you?
  I'm 10
2 How old are you?
  I'm 6
3 How old are you?
  I'm 9
4 How old are you?
  I'm 8

Ask and draw.
- Show the class the outline of the two cakes on page 26. Ask them to draw the appropriate number of candles for their own age on the first cake.
- Say *Let's work in pairs.* The pupils in each pair ask each other *How old are you?* They draw the appropriate number of candles for their partner on the second cake.
- Go round listening and checking.

Look and colour.
- Show the class the *Look and colour* activity on page 27. Point at various objects (e.g. the book, the pen) and ask *What's this?* Point at Zak and Zeeky and ask *Who's this?*
- Ask individuals to say the numbers and read the colour words in the box.
- Say *Let's colour.* Check everyone understands that they look at the numbers on the picture and refer to the colour key to check which colour to use.
- Move round the class, asking *What's this?* and *Who's this?* and pointing at things for the pupils to say the colour word in English.

My English is ...
Follow the procedure that is outlined on page 11.

Ending the lesson
Colour corners.

- Choose four of the colour flashcards and place these in the four corners of the room.
- Ask a few pupils to come the front to demonstrate playing the game. Blindfold another pupil.
- Play music for pupils to move around the room. When you stop the music, everyone chooses a corner to run to. Ask the blindfolded pupil to call out one of the colours. Anyone who is at the corner for that colour leaves the game.
- Play the game again with as many pupils as is safely possible. Change the colour for each corner regularly.

Activity Book (Optional)
If you are using the *New Chatterbox* Activity Book, use page 15 now.

Find, count and write.

Pupils count the number of candles on each cake, follow the line to the correct child and complete the child's speech bubble by writing the correct number.

Unit 4 Extra activities

How old are you? circle game
Language practised
How old are you? I'm ... .
Numbers *1–10*

Materials needed
Pieces of paper each showing number *1–10*.

- Arrange the class in a circle. Hand out a piece of paper to each pupil but ask them to keep the number secret.
- Ask the pupil next to you *How old are you?* The pupil answers giving the age on their piece of paper. (They can pretend to be that age, which will cause amusement if their paper says, e.g. *1* or *2*.)
- Continue around the circle with everyone asking their neighbour *How old are you?*

Number groups
Language practised
Numbers 1–10

- Explain to the class that you will play some music for them to dance to.
- When the music stops, say a number. The pupils organize themselves into groups of that number. (Inevitably there will be some children left over each time.)

Lesson 1

Language focus
Toys: *ball, car, teddy bear, doll, bike, guitar*
Asking and answering about toys

Classroom English
Thanks, Bye, please

Materials needed
Flashcards: *ball, car, teddy bear, doll, bike, guitar*
A cardboard box

Starting the lesson

- Say *Hello* to your class. Encourage them all to say *Hello* back to you.
- Hold up the classroom objects (bag, pen, pencil etc). Ask *What's this?* each time. The class answers
  It's a ... .
- Encourage individuals to come to the front, choose an object, hold it up and ask *What's this?* to the whole class or to another individual pupil.
- Sing the *Number Samba* song from Unit 2, Lesson 2.

Presentation

- Have ready flashcards for *ball, car, teddy bear, doll, bike* and *guitar*. Ask six pupils to stand in different places around the classroom and each hold up a flashcard.
- Point to each toy and say, e.g. *It's a doll.* The class repeats.
- Ask the six pupils to swap places with each other. Say, e.g. *It's a guitar* and ask the class to point to the guitar. Repeat the procedure a few times.

Practice (PUPIL'S BOOK p. 28)

28 Listen, point and say.

- Say *Open your books* and show page 28. Explain that Zak and Zeeky have found their way into the cupboard in a toy shop. Zak is peeping into the labelled boxes and Zeeky is asking him what everything is.
- Play the recording. The pupils listen.
  Tapescript
  Zeeky   What's this?
  Zak   It's a bike.
  Zeeky   What's this?
  Zak   It's a guitar.
  Zeeky   What's this?
  Zak   It's a doll.
  Zeeky   What's this?
  Zak   It's a teddy bear.
  Zeeky   What's this?
  Zak   It's a car

  Zeeky   What's this?
  Zak   It's a ball.

- Say *Listen, point and say*. Play the audio again and pause after each question and answer. The pupils point to the correct toy each time and repeat the answer.
- Say *Let's work in pairs*. One pupil in each pair points at a toy and asks *What's this?* The other pupil answers. Go round listening and helping.

29 Listen and answer.

- Hide one of the flashcards in the box and ask *What's this?* Encourage guesses (e.g. *It's a car.*) Repeat the procedure with other toys. You can have a small part of the picture protruding to help the children guess.
- Look at the second activity on the page. Ask the class to look at each box and silently guess what is inside.
- Play the recording. Pause before each answer to allow the pupils a chance to give their answer first. Then play the answer for them to see if they were right.
  Tapescript
  1. What's this?
     It's a ball.
  2. What's this?
     It's a guitar.
  3. What's this?
     It's a teddy bear.
  4. What's this?
     It's a bike.
  5. What's this?
     It's a doll.
  6. What's this?
     It's a car.
- Say, e.g. *Number 3. What's this?* to a few individuals. They answer.

Ask and answer.

- Say *Let's work in pairs*. One pupil in each pair points at a picture and asks *What's this?* The other pupil answers. Go round listening and helping.

30 Story (PUPIL'S BOOK p. 29)

- Say *Open your books* and show page 29.
- Ask if the class can remember what happened in the fourth episode of the story, in Unit 4: Captain Shadow and Luke found the canal boat and introduced themselves to Chocolate Chip. She unlocked the boat and they found Pluto, who, amazingly, had not eaten any of the donuts.
- Play the recording. The pupils follow in their books.

Tapescript

Captain Shadow	Bye, Chocolate Chip!
Chocolate Chip	Goodbye, Captain Shadow ... Bye, Pluto!
Pluto	Woof! Woof! Woof!
Captain Shadow	Hey, Pluto! Stop!
Luke	Oh, Pluto! Not again – please!
Captain Shadow	Come here, Pluto! BANG! BANG!
Luke	What's that?
Captain Shadow	I don't know. BANG! BANG!

- See if anyone can remember what Captain Shadow says at the beginning of this episode (*Bye, Chocolate Chip!*) Ask the pupils what *Bye* is short for.
- Play the recording again. This time encourage everyone to join in with Captain Shadow's *I don't know*.
- Play the episode right through again. Stop the tape after each line and pupils repeat it, first chorally and then individually.

Story performance

- Ask three pupils to come to the front. Play the recording. The three pupils act out the parts of Captain Shadow, Luke and Chocolate Chip. The rest of the class does the sound effects for Pluto's barking and for the banging noise.
- If time allows, ask other groups to act out the episode.

Ending the lesson

- Ask everyone to choose one of the six toys to mime.
- Say, e.g. *Goodbye, guitar*. Everyone playing the guitar stops and says *Goodbye*.
- Continue until everyone has said *Goodbye*.

Activity Book (Optional)

If you are using the *New Chatterbox* Activity Book, use page 16 now.

Colour and write.

Pupils join up the dots, colour in the completed pictures and trace the words below each picture.

Read and draw.

Pupils read the question *What's this?* and look at each picture of Zak and Zeeky playing with different objects. They read the sentences and draw the missing toys in the pictures.

Lesson 2

Language focus
Is it a ...? Yes, No
robot, bicycle
Asking and answering about objects

Materials needed
The toy flashcards, a large cloth

Starting the lesson

- Say *Hello* to the class. They reply.
- Call out the six toys from last lesson. The class does the correct mime each time.
- Ask individuals to come the front and mime one of the toys. The class calls out each time, e.g. *It's a ball*.

Presentation

- Ask a pupil to come and start drawing one of the toys on the board. Encourage them to take their time so that it is not immediately obvious what they are drawing.
- Ask, e.g. *Is it a doll? Is it a teddy bear?* The pupil answers *Yes* or *No*.
- Say *Is it a ...?* slowly for the class to repeat. Ask other pupils to come and draw toys on the board and encourage the class to ask *Is it a ...?* questions.

Practice (PUPIL'S BOOK p. 30)

Ask and answer.

- Say *Open your books* and show page 30. Say *Ask and answer*.
- Read Zak's speech bubble *Is it a teddy bear?* Elicit Sam's answer (*No*) from the class. Do the same with Anna and Suzy's speech bubbles.
- Ask the boys to read the *Is it a ...?* speech bubbles and the girls to read the *Yes* and *No* bubbles. Swap roles and repeat the procedure.
- Wrap the cloth around the guitar flashcard (or a real one if you have it). Ask two pupils to come the front. They carry out the exchange in the book with one pupil asking *Is it a teddy bear?* and the other answering *No*, the first asking *Is it a guitar?* and the other answering *Yes*.

Play.

- Say *Let's work in pairs*. In each pair the pupils take turns asking and answering the *Is it a ...?* questions.
- Hide other toy flashcards inside the cloth and elicit *Is it a ...?* questions from the class.

Look, ask and answer.
- Show the next activity. Say the number for one of the pictures and encourage individuals to ask *Is it a ...?* questions about that picture.
- Say *Let's work in pairs*. Arrange the class into pairs or small groups. They take turns asking and answering *Is it a ...?* for each picture.
- Go round listening and helping.

Song (PUPIL'S BOOK p. 31)
- Say *Open your books*. Show them page 31.
- Play the recording. The pupils listen and look at the pictures.

Tapescript
What's this? What's this?
Is it a buzz-buzz robot?
Or a zoom-zoom car?
Or a ding-ding bicycle?

Yes! It's a bicycle!

What's this? What's this?
Is it a boom-boom ball?
Or a beep-beep robot?
Or a ding-ding bicycle?

Yes! It's a robot!

What's this? What's this?
Is it a zoom-zoom car?
Or a boom-boom ball?
Or a ding-ding bicycle?

Yes! It's a ball!

- Ask a group of pupils to come to the front. Play the recording again. Everyone joins in and the group at the front calls out the answer at the end of each verse.

Song performance
- Play the recording again. Everyone sings along and the pupils create sound effects at the right moments.

Ending the lesson
- Do a quick review of colours and numbers. Count 1–10 around the class. Every time they reach 10 hold one of the colour flashcards and elicit the colour word from the whole class.
- Do a quick review of actions. Call out *Stand up, Look, Listen, Sit down, Open your books, Close your books*. Ask small groups to carry out the instructions each time and then say *Goodbye*.
- Continue until you have said *Goodbye* to each group.

Activity Book (Optional)
If you are using the *New Chatterbox* Activity Book, use page 17 now.

✓ **the correct pictures.**
Pupils look at each pair of pictures and tick the picture that is the same as in the story in the Pupil's Book. The other picture has got small differences.

Lesson 3

Language focus
Unit 5 revision
Practising and consolidating the language
Starting to recognize and read familiar words

Classroom English
Is that right?

Materials needed
Flashcards: *car, bike, teddy bear, ball, doll, guitar*
Simple word cards for *car, bike, teddy bear, ball, doll, guitar*

Starting the lesson
- Greet the class as usual. Hold up the flashcards one by one, each time asking *What's this?* The class or individuals reply *It's a ...* .
- Ask six pupils to come the front and ask each of them to hold up one of the flashcards.
- Hold up one of the word cards, e.g. *doll*. Ask *What's this?* Help the class read the word if necessary.
- Ask a pupil to take the word card and hold it up next to the pupil who is holding the doll flashcard.
- Repeat the procedure with the other five cards.

Practice (PUPIL'S BOOK pp. 31–32)
Look and write ✓ or ✗.
- Draw a ball on the board and ask *Is it a ball?*
- Write the word *guitar* under the picture of the ball. Look worried and ask *Is that right?* Use gesture to help explain your question and elicit the answer *No* from the class.
- Now write the word *ball* under the picture of the ball. Ask *Is that right?* and elicit the answer *Yes*.
- Say *Open your books* and show page 32. Ask *Is it a ball?* about the first picture then demonstrate tracing the line with your finger to the word *teddy bear*.
- Ask *Is that right?* When the class answers *No*, demonstrate writing a cross in the box next to the word.
- Go round checking and helping as the class continues the activity individually.

- Check the activity as a class. Ask *Is it a ...?* for each picture, then write the word at the end of the line on the board. Ask *Is that right?* for the class to answer *Yes* or *No* each time.

Choose and draw.
- Show the class the activity on page 33. Point out the word pool at the top of the page and ask individuals to read the words in the box. Show the class that *bike* has been drawn in the first box.
- Ask the class to choose three other words and draw them in the boxes.

Ask and answer.
- Say *Let's work in pairs*. Ask one pair to demonstrate, with one pupil asking *What's this?* and the other answering *It's a bike* for the first picture. The class continues the activity in their pairs.
- Go round listening and checking.

My English is ...
Follow the procedure that is outlined on page 11.

Ending the lesson
- Sing the *Ding-ding bicycle* song from Lesson 2. Hand out the toy flashcards and ask pupils to hold them up at the relevant moments.
- Say *Goodbye* to the class.

Activity Book (Optional)
If you are using the *New Chatterbox* Activity Book, use page 18 now.

Look and ✓ or ✗.
Pupils look at the picture, read the questions and tick or cross the box under each question.

Unit 5 Extra activities

Drawing charades
Language practised
Is it a ...? Yes, No, toys

Materials needed
Paper and pencils for each group

- Arrange the class into small groups. Ask one pupil from each group to come up to you. Tell them or show them a toy word. They return to their group and start drawing the toy.
- Other members of the group ask, e.g. *Is it a teddy bear?* The pupil who is drawing, answers *Yes* or *No*.
- When the group has guessed correctly they send another member to you to tell you the correct word. You give them a new toy word to draw.

Memory game
Language practised
Toys, colours

Materials needed
A tray, the six toy flashcards the class knows, six pieces of coloured card (red, white, green, blue, black, yellow), a large cloth

- Place all the toy flashcards on the tray. Allow the class time to look at them all.
- Cover the tray with the cloth. Working in pairs or small groups, pupils try to remember all the six toy flashcards that were on the tray. They whisper the words to each other or draw pictures of the items.
- Ask one group to list the items. Ask other pupils to add any which have been forgotten.
- Repeat the procedure with the pieces of coloured card, or use the toy flashcards again but take one away so that the pupils have to remember which ones were there.

Unit 6

Lesson 1

Language focus
More colours: *pink, brown, orange, purple, grey*
Revising and learning more colours

Classroom English
Don't forget …

Materials needed
Flashcards: *white, green, black, yellow, red, blue, pink, brown, orange, purple, grey*
If possible, pink, brown, orange, purple and grey chalk or board pens
Large splodges cut from pink, brown, orange, purple and grey paper or card

---

Starting the lesson

- Say *Hello* to your class. Encourage them all to say *Hello* back to you.
- Hand out the flashcards for *red, blue, green, yellow, black* and *white*.
- Say a colour word. The pupil with the colour you say jumps up and down, then gives their colour to another pupil.
- Continue the procedure, gaining speed.
- Sing the *Ding-ding bicycle* song from Unit 5, Lesson 2.

Presentation

- Have ready the flashcards for *pink, brown, orange, purple* and *grey*. Ask five pupils to stand in different places around the classroom and hold up their flashcard.
- Point to each flashcard and say the colour word. The class repeats.
- Ask the five pupils to swap places with each other. Say the colour words again and ask the class to point to the colours as you say them. Repeat the procedure a few times.

Practice (PUPIL'S BOOK p. 34)

32 Listen, point and say.

- Say *Open your books* and show page 34.
- Play the recording. Pupils listen.
  Tapescript
  orange, grey, pink, brown, purple
- Say *Listen, point and say*. Play the recording again and pause after each colour. The pupils point to the right paint pot and all the related coloured drips each time. They also repeat the colour word.
- Say *Let's work in pairs*. Play the recording again. Pupils take turns in their pair or small groups pointing and saying the colour word with the recording.

33 Listen and colour.

- Draw some paint blobs on the board and number them.
- Say, e.g. *3 is pink*. If you have a piece of pink chalk or a pink board pen, ask a pupil to colour the Number 3 blob. If you do not have suitable pens the pupil points to Number 3 blob and holds up the pink flashcard.
- Repeat the procedure involving other pupils and colours.
- Play the recording. Pause after each line. Play each line again for the pupils to colour the right paint brush and drips. Go round helping where necessary.
  Tapescript
  1 purple.
  2 orange.
  3 brown.
  4 grey.
  5 pink.
- When everyone is ready check the activity together. Play the recording again to check.
- After each sentence ask two pupils to come to the front and hold up the right number card and the correctly coloured flashcard, or to colour a numbered blob on the board if you have suitable chalk or pens.

34 Story (PUPIL'S BOOK p. 35)

- Say *Open your books* and show page 35.
- Ask if the class can remember what happened in the fifth episode of the story, in Unit 5: Pluto heard urgent banging coming from inside one of the factories along the canal bank. He and Captain Shadow went to investigate the noise.
- Play the recording. The pupils follow in their books.
  Tapescript
	BANG! BANG!
Zoko	Help!
Luke	Is it a ghost?
Captain Shadow	No, Luke. It's a robot.
Zoko	Yes, I'm DJ's robot. Help!
Captain Shadow	Ready, Pluto? 1 – 2 – 3!
Pluto	Woof!
Captain Shadow	Hello. What's your name?
Zoko	I'm Zoko.
Pluto	Woof!
Zoko	Hello, Pluto – thank you!
Pluto	Woof!
- Play the recording again. This time everyone joins in with Zoko's words.
- Play the episode right through again. Stop the tape after each line and pupils repeat it, first chorally and then individually.

Story performance
- Ask three pupils to come to the front. Play the recording. The three pupils act out the parts of Captain Shadow, Luke and Zoko. The rest of the class does the sound effects for Pluto barking and for the banging.
- If time allows, ask other groups to act out the episode.

Ending the lesson
- Explain you will say a colour. Anyone wearing anything in that colour stands up, moves to the door and says *Goodbye*.
- Continue until everyone has said *Goodbye*.

Activity Book (Optional)
If you are using the *New Chatterbox* Activity Book, use page 19 now.

Colour.
Pupils read the colour on the paint tin and colour it the same colour.

Find, circle and colour.
Pupils find and circle a colour in each line. Then they follow the line to the object and colour the object in that colour.

Lesson 2

Language focus
What colour is it? It's …
Asking and answering about colour

Materials needed
Flashcards: *pink, purple, grey, orange* and *brown*
Familiar objects (e.g. toys and classroom objects) in familiar colours
A large backing sheet for each group, glue, scissors, all sorts of materials in the target colours, e.g. wool, scraps of material, plastic wrapping, glitter, catalogues and magazines containing plenty of colour etc.

Starting the lesson
- Say *Hello* to the class. They reply.
- Hold up the colour flashcards from Lesson 1. The pupils call out the colours.
- Divide the class into five groups, one for each colour. Say, e.g. *Stand up, purple*. The pupils in the purple group all stand up. Continue with, e.g. *Open your books, brown; Listen, grey* etc.
- Continue the procedure, this time dividing the class into eleven groups so that you can revise the six colours (*red, blue, green, yellow, black, white*) from Unit 3 too.

Presentation
- Hold up a familiar object in a familiar colour (e.g. a blue book). Ask *What's this?* (*It's a book.*) Then ask *What colour is it?* Help with the answer *It's blue*.
- Continue this procedure, involving as many pupils and different coloured objects as possible.

Practice (PUPIL'S BOOK p. 36)
Listen and point.
- Say *Open your books* and show page 36. Play the recording and encourage pupils to look at the pictures and point to the person that is speaking. Ask why Zeeky is feeling guilty.

Tapescript
Sam   What colour is it?
Zeeky   It's purple.

- Say *Ask and answer*. Ask all the boys to read the Sam's speech bubble and all the girls to answer as Zeeky.
- Swap the roles and repeat until the class is confident at asking the new question.
- Ask a boy and girl to come the front with a book. The boy points to the objects in the picture and asks *What colour is it?* Encourage him to sound shocked at the mess. The girl answers as Zeeky, rather apologetically.

Ask and answer.
- Say *Let's work in pairs*. In each pair one pupil points at an object and asks *What colour is it?* in a shocked voice. The other pupil answers apologetically.
- Go round listening and helping.

Colour and say.
- Show the next activity. Explain that the pupils will colour the words in the right colour.
- Go around looking at the pupils' work, pointing and asking *What colour is it?*

- **Make a colour collage.** Organise the class into up to eleven groups. Give each group a colour. Write these on the board.
- Give each group a large backing sheet. A volunteer from each group writes their colour word on the sheet in the appropriate colour.
- Lay out all the materials for making the collages. Ask the groups to come and select the material and paints in the appropriate colour for their group. Encourage them to cut out pictures or parts of pictures in the appropriate colours from magazines and catalogues.
- Encourage the groups first to arrange and then to stick the material onto the backing sheet to make an attractive collage.

🔊 Song (PUPIL'S BOOK p. 37)

- Say *Open your books* and show page 37.
- Play the recording. The pupils listen and look at the pictures.

Tapescript
Grass is green
And clouds are grey
And the sun is yellow!

Earth is brown
And snow is white
And the sun is yellow!

Grass is green
And sky is blue
And the sun is yellow!

- Play the song again. This time the class calls out the colour word each time along with the music.
- Hand out the colour flashcards that are mentioned in the song to individual pupils. Play the song again. The pupils with flashcards hold them up while the class calls out the colour.

Song performance

- Agree actions for *grass, clouds, sun, earth, snow, sun, grass* and *sky*.
- Play the recording again. This time everyone sings along and does the actions.

Ending the lesson

- Revise *How old are you?* Ask a pupil *How old are you?* Tell them not to reply, but instead to jump the appropriate number of times for their age. They then say *I'm ...*, pause, and wait for the class to supply the number.
- Repeat the procedure with a few pupils.
- Ask a pupil *How old are you?* They reply, e.g. *I'm 6*. Say *Stand up*. Encourage all the other 6 year olds to stand up and repeat *I'm 6*.
- Say *Goodbye* to all the 6 year olds. They reply *Goodbye* and move towards the door.
- Repeat the procedure with all the other age groups in the class.

Activity Book (Optional)

If you are using the *New Chatterbox* Activity Book, use page 20 now.

Read and circle.

Pupils look at the picture carefully to see which story character it is in each picture. Then they circle the correct sentence below each picture, according to who they think it is.

Lesson 3

Language focus
Unit 6 revision

Function
Practising and consolidating the language

Materials needed
Flashcards: *green, white, brown, grey, yellow, blue*
Familiar toys and classroom objects in familiar colours

Starting the lesson

- Greet the class as usual. Hold up familiar toys and classroom objects asking *What's this?* each time.
- Continue by asking *What colour is it?*
- Encourage individuals to come to the front and name another pupil. The first pupil chooses an object and asks the pupil they have named *What's this?* and *What colour is it?* The named pupil answers and then comes to the front and chooses another object and pupil to ask.

Practice (PUPIL'S BOOK pp. 38–39)

Look and colour.

- Say *Open your books* and show page 38.
- Ask individuals to say the colour words working down the page.
- Demonstrate following the first line and asking *What's this?* when you reach the guitar. Then demonstrate colouring the guitar in the colour at the beginning of the line (red).
- Ask the class to complete the activity in the same way. Go round pointing and asking *What's this?* and *What colour is it?*

Ask and answer.

- Say *Let's work in pairs*. The children in each pair ask each other *What's this?* and *What colour is it?* working down the line of pictures.
- Go round listening and checking.

Play and say.

- Draw a simple 5 x 5 grid on the board, with numbers 1–5 down the left side and 6–10 along the bottom.
- Give a reference, e.g. *1, 9* and ask a pupil to come and draw a cross in the appropriate square. Repeat this until you feel the class is confident about how to find a grid reference.
- Show the class the *Play and say* activity on page 39. Ask a pupil to read Zak's speech bubble *2, 7*. Ask everyone to find the correct box and give the answer (Zeeky's bubble) *It's a bike*.
- Call out more references for the class to find, each time giving the answer *It's a ...* .

- Ask pupils to give grid references for the rest of the class to find.
- Say *Let's work in pairs*. The pupils in each pair take turns giving a grid reference and finding the correct box (*It's a …*).
- Go round listening and helping.

My English is …
Follow the procedure that is outlined on page 11.

- **Guess the object.** Arrange the class into a circle and place familiar objects in familiar colours in the centre.
- Ask everyone secretly to choose an object.
- Pick a pupil and try to guess their object by asking, e.g. *Is it a book? Is it a ball?* When the pupil answers *Yes*, ask *What colour is it?* You then pick up the object.
- Check with the pupil that it is the right one, then return it and ask another pupil to guess someone else's object.

Ending the lesson
- Sing *The sun is yellow* song, from Lesson 2. Encourage the class to do the actions and hand out the flashcards for *green, white, brown, grey, yellow* and *blue* for pupils to hold up at the right moments.
- Say *Goodbye* to the class.

Activity Book (Optional)
If you are using the *New Chatterbox* Activity Book, use page 21 now.

Colour.
Pupils look at the key and colour each section in the picture in the colour that is indicated in the key to reveal the hidden picture of a doll.

Answer the question.
Pupils look at the question below the picture and complete the answer by writing in the word *doll*.

Unit 6 Extra activities

Secret pictures
Language practised
Is it a …? Yes, No
What colour is it? It's …

Materials needed
A piece of paper for each pupil, colouring pens

- Give each pupil a piece of paper and ask them to draw an object the class knows in English (e.g. a toy or classroom object). Ask them to colour it in a familiar colour.
- Everyone folds their picture so that it can't be seen and passes it around the class until you say *Stop!*
- Ask a pupil to unfold their picture. Encourage other pupils to guess the picture by asking, e.g. *Is it a guitar?* The pupil who guesses the object correctly then asks *What colour is it?*
- Play the game several times to involve as many pupils as possible.

Word groups
Language practised
Colours, numbers *1–10*, toys, classroom objects

- Explain to the class that you will say the name for a word group (e.g. Colours, Numbers, Toys, Classroom) and they have to think of as many words as they can which fit into that group.
- Start by saying, e.g. *Toys* then count *1–10* with the class. Everyone who can think of a toy word puts up their hand to say their word.
- When all the toy words have been said choose a new category and count *1–10* with the class again.

Colour corners
Language practised
Colours

Materials needed
Flashcards: *pink, brown, orange, purple, grey, red, blue, green, yellow, black* and *white*

- Choose four of the flashcards and place these in the four corners of the room.
- Play music for pupils to move around the room. When you stop the music, call out a colour. Everyone moves to the appropriate corner. The last person to reach the corner leaves the game.
- Change the colours and play the game again.

 (PUPIL'S BOOK p. 40)

Extra language
Here's your present, How old are you? I'm (age)

Materials needed
A large sheet of card or thick paper with outline of the age chart (see Pupil's Book page 40) copied onto it, dice for each pair of pupils, a counter for each pupil

(37) Listen, read and match.

- Say *Open your books* and show page 40. Allow the pupils time to look at the photos and work out what is going on.
- Play the recording. It is still unlikely at this stage that the class will be able to follow all the words in their books, but they may be able to work out which photo is being referred to.

Tapescript
1	**Mum & Dad**	Happy Birthday! Here's your present.
	Ben	Thank you!
2	Ben	What is it?
3	Ben	It's fantastic. Thank you!

- Read each speech bubble again. Ask the class to point to and say the number for the corresponding photo.

Make a chart.

- Draw attention to the chart at the bottom of page 40. Read the speech bubbles.
- Ask individuals *How old are you?* Encourage them to reply *I'm (age)*.
- Hand out a sheet of paper to each pupil and ask them to draw a chart like the one at the bottom of the Pupil's Book page.
- When pupils have finished their chart, they can go around the class asking other pupils *How old are you?* When pupils reply, e.g. *I'm 8*, they should draw a circle in the column.

Ending the lesson

- Check if it is anyone's birthday in the near future. Loosely wrap some real toys or toy flashcards and ask individuals to offer them to the 'birthday child',
- As they offer them they say *Happy Birthday! Here's your present*. The 'birthday child' says *It's fantastic! Thank you!*
- After as many pupils as possible have had a turn say *Goodbye* to the whole class.

Activity Book (Optional)
If you are using the *New Chatterbox* Activity Book, use page 22 now.

Colour the birthday pictures.
Pupils look at the pictures and only colour in the pictures of things that you have on your birthday/at a birthday party.

Draw and ✓
Pupils look at the list and draw one of the items in the empty frame. Then they tick the box next to the word for the item they have drawn.

 (PUPIL'S BOOK p. 41)

Play the game.

- Say *Open your books* and show page 41. Ask individuals to name the items in the circles.
- Make sure everyone knows where to find the stickers for the game – in the sticker insert in the middle of the book.
- Arrange the class into pairs or small groups. Explain how to play the game.
  1. Start at the start sign and throw a dice.
  2. Count round the course according to the number you throw.
  3. Name the item or colour in the balloon you land on. If you say the word correctly (your partner or other group members or your teacher will say if it is correct) find the corresponding sticker and stick it on.
  4. Take turns to throw until you have landed on all the balloons and have covered them all with stickers. Once you have been round once, carry on round again and again.

Test
Ask pupils to do Test 2.

Lesson 1

Language focus
I'm ... You're ... big, small, hungry, thirsty
Describing feelings

Classroom English
How are you? I'm fine, thank you

Materials needed
Flashcards: *1–4, big, small, hungry, thirsty*

Starting the lesson
- Say *Hello* to your class. Encourage them all to say *Hello* back to you.
- Review *I'm ...* by introducing yourself *I'm ... (name)* and encouraging pupils to introduce themselves to each other.
- Sing *The sun is yellow* song from Unit 6, Lesson 2.

Presentation
- Display the flashcards around the room. Point to each one, say the word for the class to repeat and do an appropriate action (e.g. stretch out your arms for *big*, curl up small for *small*, touch your throat and look thirsty for *thirsty* and rub your stomach and look hungry for *hungry*).
- Point to the flashcards in turn, say the word and encourage the class to do the action.
- Point to each flashcard and encourage the class to say the word.

Practice (PUPIL'S BOOK p. 42)

(39) Listen, point and say.
- Say *Open your books* and show page 42.
- Say *Listen, point and say*. Play the recording. Pupils listen.
  Tapescript
  Anna You're big.
  Zeeky I'm small.
  Sam   I'm hungry.
  Suzy I'm thirsty.
- Play the recording again and pause after each line. The pupils point to the correct character each time. They also repeat the line.
- Check that the class understands why Zeeky and Zak appear small and big in the mirrors. (They are special uneven mirrors which distort the image. Because of the often amusing images produced, these sort of mirrors are often found at funfairs.)
- Divide the class into four groups, one group for each speaker. Play the recording again. The groups join in with their speakers.

(40) Listen and join.
- Draw attention to the pictures at the bottom of the page. Explain that the class should draw lines to link each number with the appropriate picture.
- Play the recording. Pause after each line for the pupils to draw their line. Go round helping and clarifying where necessary.
  Tapescript
  1. Small.
  2. Thirsty.
  3. Big.
  4. Hungry.
- When everyone is ready check the activity together. Play the recording again. After each sentence ask two pupils to come to the front and hold up the right number flashcard and the right adjective flashcard.
- **Guess the flashcard.** Clear a large space in the classroom. Place the four adjective flashcards face down in the centre.
- Ask a volunteer to pick up a flashcard and secretly look at it. They then act out the adjective. The rest of the class makes suggestions, e.g. *You're big, You're hungry*.
- Whoever guesses the adjective then picks up another flashcard and acts it out.

(41) Story (PUPIL'S BOOK p. 43)
- Say *Open your books* and show page 43.
- Ask if the class can remember what happened in the sixth episode of the story in Unit 6: Pluto and Captain Shadow managed to pull Zoko out of the vat of donut icing, using Pluto's lead.
- Play the recording. Pupils listen and follow in their books.
  Tapescript
  Captain Shadow Hello, Zoko! How are you?
  Zoko   I'm fine, Captain. Here's a message from Chocolate Chip.
  Zoko   Is it bad, Captain?
  Captain Shadow It's not good, Zoko. Donut Joe is missing!
  Captain Shadow (reading) Dear Captain Shadow, Donut Joe is missing. Please find him! Your friend, Chocolate Chip.
  Captain Shadow Right! Come on, Luke. Let's find DJ!
  Pluto   Woof! Woof!
  Zoko   OK, Pluto. Let's go to the park.
- Ask if anyone can guess what *How are you?* means. What is the normal reply? (*I'm fine, thank you*). Practise the question and answer all together and then ask individuals *How are you?* They answer *I'm fine, thank you*.
- Play the recording again. This time everyone joins in with *How are you?* and *I'm fine*.

- Play the episode right through again. Stop the tape after each line and pupils repeat it, first chorally and then individually.

Story performance
- Ask two pupils to come to the front. Play the recording. The two pupils act out the parts of Captain Shadow and Zoko, supported by the recording. The rest of the class does the sound effects for Pluto's barking.
- If time allows, ask other pairs to act out the episode.

Ending the lesson
- Place the four adjective flashcards in different corners of the room. Ask everyone to go to a corner. They act out the adjective in their corner.
- Say one of the adjectives, e.g. *thirsty*. All the pupils in the thirsty corner say *Goodbye* and move the door.
- Continue until everyone has said *Goodbye*.

Activity Book (Optional)
If you are using the *New Chatterbox* Activity Book, use page 23 now.

Read and ✓ the correct sentences.
Pupils look at the pictures and tick the boxes next to the correct description for each picture.

Match.
Pupils look at the pictures and match the speech bubbles to their speakers.

Lesson 2

Language focus
He's ..., She's ..., happy, sad, big, small, hungry, thirsty
Describing how others are feeling

Classroom English
good, bad

Materials needed
Flashcards: *happy, sad, big, small, hungry, thirsty*

Starting the lesson
- Say *Hello* to the class and ask *How are you?* Encourage the answer *I'm fine, thank you*.
- Hold up the six adjective flashcards. The pupils call out the words.
- Distribute the flashcards to six pupils. Ask the pupils with cards to hold them up and say, e.g. *I'm sad*.
- Continue the procedure, involving as many pupils as possible.

Presentation (PUPIL'S BOOK p. 44)
(42) Listen, point and say.
- Ask six pupils to come to the front and give each of them a flashcard to hold up. Encourage them to act out their adjective.
- Point to each pupil and say, e.g. *He's happy, She's thirsty*.
- Say *Open your books* and show page 44. Say *Listen, point and say*.
- Play the recording. The class repeats each line and points at the happy girl on the rollercoaster and the sad boy who has dropped his ice cream.
Tapescript
He's sad.
She's happy.

Practice
Look and write.
- Ask different pupils to read the words in the coloured boxes.
- Ask the class to work in pairs to decide which words are needed for each picture. When they are ready they write the words they have chosen on the lines.
- Go round checking and helping.

(43) Song (PUPIL'S BOOK p. 45)
- Say *Open your books* and show page 45.
- Play the recording. The pupils listen and look at the pictures.
Tapescript
Happy Clown is yellow
Black Clown is sad
Good Clown is white
Blue Clown is bad
What colour is Happy Clown?
What colour is Sad?
What colour is Good Clown?
What colour is Bad?
- Check that everyone understands *good* and *bad*.
- Explain that *Good, Bad, Happy* and *Sad* are describing the different coloured clowns in the picture. Ask individuals *What colour is Happy?* etc.
- Play the first verse of the song again. This time the class calls out the colour words.
- Play the second verse and pause at the end of each line. Allow individuals to call out the colours.

Ending the lesson
- Ask small groups of pupils to take slow steps towards the door. As they take each step, say *big, small, happy* or *sad*. The pupils act out the adjective you say as they take each step.
- Repeat the procedure until everyone is at the door.

Activity Book (Optional)
If you are using the New Chatterbox Activity Book, use page 24 now.

Number and colour.
Pupils number the story pictures in the same order they appear in the Pupil's Book and then colour them in.

Lesson 3

Language focus
Unit 7 revision

Function
Practising and consolidating the language

Materials needed
Flashcards: *big, small, hungry, thirsty, happy, sad*

Starting the lesson
- Greet the class as usual. Ask *How are you?* to individuals. They reply *I'm fine, thank you*.
- Give individual pupils flashcards for *happy* or *sad*. Ask them *How are you?* Encourage them to reply *I'm happy / sad*. Say to the rest of the class *He's / She's happy / sad*.
- Continue the procedure, this time encouraging pupils to say *He's / She's happy / sad*.

Practice (PUPIL'S BOOK pp. 46–47)

Read, join and say.
- Say *Open your books* and show page 46. Say *Read, join and say*.
- Ask individuals to read the descriptions at the top of the picture. Show them how to find people in the picture to fit the descriptions. They draw lines linking each description to the right person.

Write and say.
- Say *Let's work in pairs*. The pairs agree which adjective to use for each speech bubble and write the words on the lines.
- The pairs take turns reading the speech bubbles to each other.
- Go round listening and checking. Check the activity by asking individuals to read out each speech bubble to the rest of the class.

Then draw, write and say.
- The pupils draw a picture of themselves looking happy, sad, big, small, thirsty or hungry. They write the appropriate adjective on the line.
- Ask different pupils to hold up their picture and read out their speech bubble.

My English is …
Follow the procedure that is outlined on page 11.

He and She.
- Arrange the class into a circle, ideally alternating between girl and boy.
- Move round the circle gesturing to each pair and saying, e.g. *She's big. He's small*. The girl and boy must try to act the correct adjective. This will help them learn to listen out for and distinguish between *He* and *She*.
- Repeat the procedure several times, gathering speed as the pupils gain confidence.

Ending the lesson
- Sing the *Colour clowns* song from Lesson 2. Encourage the class to do the actions and give different pupils turns to call out the colours they like in verse 2.
- Say *Goodbye* to the class.

Activity Book (Optional)
If you are using the *New Chatterbox* Activity Book, use page 25 now.

Write He's or She's.
Pupils look at the pictures and complete the sentences with *He's* or *She's*.

Look and complete.
Pupils look at the pictures and then complete the crossword with the correct words.

Unit 7 Extra activities

I'm happy, She's happy

Language practised
I'm ... He's ... She's ... happy, sad, hungry, thirsty

- Arrange the class in a circle. Ask a pupil to start by saying, e.g. *I'm hungry*. The next pupil gestures to the first pupil and says to the rest of the class *He's / She's hungry*.
- The second pupil then points to themselves and says, e.g. *I'm sad*. The next pupil gestures to this pupil and says to the rest of the class *He's / She's sad*. The challenge is to use *He's* and *She's* correctly.
- Continue round the circle, or call out names across the circle to keep everyone interested.

Funny pictures

Language practised
You're ... big, small, happy, sad, thirsty, hungry

Materials needed
A piece of paper and pencil for each pupil

- Give each pupil a piece of paper and ask them to draw themselves looking big, small, happy, sad, thirsty or hungry. The pictures can be as amusing as the pupils wish as long as the adjective is clear.
- Ask an individual to show their picture to the rest of the class. The class choruses, e.g. *You're hungry*.
- Everyone shows their picture to their neighbour who says, e.g. *You're small*.

Unit 8

Lesson 1

Language focus
Pets: *hamster, rabbit, cat, dog, fish, bird*
Identifying and presenting pets

Classroom English
What's wrong?

Materials needed
Flashcards: *hamster, rabbit, cat, dog, fish, bird, numbers 1–4*
Classroom items, a soft ball

Starting the lesson

- Say *Hello* to your class. Ask a few individuals *How are you?*
- Review *What's this? It's a ...* . Hold up a classroom item, e.g. a book and ask *What's this?* The class replies *It's a book*.
- Ask different pupils to hold up other classroom items and ask *What's this?* Choose individuals to reply.
- Sing the *Colour clowns* song from Unit 7, Lesson 2.

Presentation

- Display the six pet flashcards around the room.
- Point to each flashcard and say the word for the class to repeat.
- Say the six pets again. Encourage the class to repeat the word and point to the right flashcard each time.
- Say the six pets. This time encourage the class to do a suitable action or make a noise for each one.

Practice (PUPIL'S BOOK p. 48)

(44) Listen, point and say.

- Say *Open your books* and show page 48.
- Play the recording. The pupils listen.
  Tapescript
  Girl 1: This is my rabbit.
  Girl 2: This is my cat.
  Boy 1: This is my fish.
  Girl 3: This is my hamster.
  Boy 2: This is my dog.
  Girl 4: This is my bird.
- Say *Listen, point and say*. Play the recording again and pause after each line. The pupils point to the correct pet each time. They also repeat the line.
- Say the six pet words in random order. The class mimes or makes a noise each time.

(45) Listen and number.

- Show the pictures along the bottom of the Pupil's Book page and ask volunteers to call out the pet words.
- Play the recording. Ask the pupils to point to the appropriate picture each time.
- Play the recording again. This time pupils write the correct number next to each pet.

Tapescript
1. Cat.
2. Rabbit.
3. Fish.
4. Bird.

- When everyone is ready check the activity together. Play the recording.
- After each sentence ask two pupils to come to the front and hold up the correct number flashcard and the correct pet flashcard. Check any misunderstandings.

- **Roll a ball.** Clear a space in the classroom. Place the six pet flashcards face up on the floor.
- Demonstrate rolling a soft ball onto (or nearly onto) one of the flashcards. Hold up the flashcard nearest to the ball and say, e.g. *This is my rabbit.*
- Allow as many pupils as possible to have a turn at rolling the ball and picking up one of the flashcards.

(46) Story (PUPIL'S BOOK p. 49)

- Say *Open your books* and show them page 49.
- Ask if the class can remember what happened in the seventh episode of the story, in Unit 7: Zoko came to see Captain Shadow and Luke with a message from Chocolate Chip to say that Donut Joe had gone missing. Captain Shadow agreed to help find him, but first Pluto went to play in the park with Zoko.
- Play the recording. The pupils follow in their books.

Tapescript
Zoko What's wrong, Pluto?
Zoko Stop, Pluto!
Pluto Woof!
Zoko What's wrong, Pluto? Is Donut Joe here?
Pluto Woof!
Zoko I've got an idea, Pluto. Let's watch the café.

- Ask if anyone can guess what *What's wrong?* means. Say the question for the class to repeat.
- Whisper to a few pupils to pretend to be upset or hurt. Encourage other pupils to go up to them and ask gently *What's wrong?*
- Play the recording again. This time everyone joins in with Zoko's *What's wrong, Pluto?*

- Play the episode right through again. Stop after each line and pupils repeat it, first chorally and then individually.

Story performance

- Ask two pupils to come to the front. Play the recording. The pupils act out the parts of Zoko and Pluto, supported by the recording.
- If time allows, ask other pairs to act out the episode.

Ending the lesson

- Place the six pet flashcards where everyone can see them. Ask everyone secretly to choose a pet.
- Ask a pupil to remove one of the flashcards. Say, e.g. *Goodbye, hamster.* Everyone who had chosen the hamster, gets up, moves towards the door and says *Goodbye.*
- Continue until everyone has said *Goodbye.*

Activity Book (Optional)

If you are using the *New Chatterbox* Activity Book, use page 26 now.

Find, circle and match.

Pupils find and circle each animal in the wordsnake and draw a line from the word to the correct picture.

Look and write.

Pupils look at the picture, find the number on each animal and complete the corresponding sentences with the name of the animal.

Lesson 2

Language focus
I've got a ... cat, dog, bird, fish, hamster, rabbit
Talking about possession

Materials needed
Flashcards: cat, dog, bird, fish, hamster, rabbit
A photo of one of the above

Starting the lesson
- Greet the class as usual.
- Hold up the six pet flashcards. The pupils call out the words.
- Distribute the flashcards to six pupils. Ask the pupils with cards to hold them up and ask *What's this?* The class replies, e.g. *It's a rabbit*.
- Continue the procedure, involving as many pupils as possible.

Presentation
- Hold up your photo of one of the pets the pupils know in English. Say, e.g. *I've got a cat*.
- Hold up one of the flashcards and say, e.g. *I've got a fish*. Say the sentence again, slowly, for the class to repeat.
- Repeat the procedure with the other five flashcards each time helping with the new language *I've got a ...* and leaving the class to complete the sentence by saying the pet.

Practice (PUPIL'S BOOK p. 50)
47 Listen, look and say.
- Say *Open your books* and show page 50. Say *Look, listen and say*. Explain that the class will hear children talking about their pets and they will call out the correct picture number each time.
- Play the recording. Pause after each line for the class to point to the correct picture and say the number.

Tapescript
1. Girl: I've got a rabbit.
2. Suzy: I've got a hamster.
3. Sam: I've got a dog.
4. Anna: I've got a cat.
5. Boy: I've got a bird.

Look and write.
- Ask pupils to look at the pictures at the bottom of the page. Can they spot the pets?
- Ask individuals to complete the speech bubbles orally for each picture. Then ask everyone to write the words onto the lines.
- Go round checking and helping.

48 Song (PUPIL'S BOOK p. 51)
- Say *Open your books* and show page 51.
- Play the recording of *Pluto's song*. The pupils listen and look at the pictures.

Tapescript
You're a fish
Bubble – bubble
I'm a dog
Woof – woof!
You're a rabbit
Hop – hop!
I'm a dog
Woof – woof!
You're a cat
Mi – aow!
I'm a dog
Woof – woof!
I'm Plu-to!

- Divide the class into two groups, one to sing the words and one to do the sound effects *Bubble-bubble*, *Hop-hop*! etc. and play the song again.
- Play the song again. This time ask four pupils to hold up the pet flashcards at the right moments. Everyone else does actions for each pet as it is mentioned.

Ending the lesson
- Ask everyone secretly to choose a pet.
- Say, e.g. *Goodbye, cats*. The pupils who chose cats make their way to the door in the manner of a cat, e.g. miaowing and prowling.
- Repeat the procedure until everyone is at the door.

Activity Book (Optional)
If you are using the *New Chatterbox* Activity Book, use page 27 now.

✓ **the correct pictures.**

Pupils look at each pair of pictures and tick the picture that is the same as in the story in the Pupil's Book. The other picture has got small differences.

Lesson 3

Language focus
Unit 8 revision

Function
Practising and consolidating the language

Classroom English
Toy, pet

Materials needed
Flashcards: *ball, guitar, bike, doll, car, teddy bear, cat, dog, bird, fish, rabbit, hamster*
Word cards: the above words written in large letters on a piece of paper

Starting the lesson

- Greet the class as usual. Ask *How are you?* to individuals. They reply *I'm fine, thank you*.
- Do a quick review of toy vocabulary by holding up the flashcards and asking *What's this?* Encourage replies using *It's a …* .
- Ask the class to pass round the toy and pet flashcards until you say *Stop*. The pupils with cards hold them up and say, e.g. *I've got a car*.

Practice (PUPIL'S BOOK pp. 52–53)

Write and colour.

- Say *Open your books* and show page 52. Say *Write and colour*.
- Ask individuals to read the descriptions under each picture, adding the word for the pet. Explain to the class that they will colour each picture according to the colour in the description.
- They then complete the description by writing the word for the pet in the picture.
- Check the activity with the class and then ask them to choose a pet to draw in the final frame. They choose a colour to use and then complete the description writing in the pet and the colour.

Look and say.

- Show the class the game on page 53. Explain that the children and Zak and Zeeky are playing a game in which they each have either a picture or a word card with pictures of toys, animals and classroom items. They are trying to find their partner by going around and saying, e.g. *I've got a guitar*. If the card they choose is the corresponding word or picture card, they say *Snap!* If, not, they say *No* and move on. The aim is to find their partners.
- Read the speech bubbles on the page until the class is confident with saying them.

Find your partner.

- Then give each pupil a word card or a picture card. Make sure that there is a flashcard and a word card for each vocabulary item. Children go around the room, saying, e.g. *I've got a dog* and trying to find their partner.
- When the game has been played a sufficient number of times, show the class Zeeky's speech bubble and ask volunteers what it should say.
- Ask everyone to complete the speech bubble. Go round asking individuals to read the completed speech bubble to you.

My English is …

Follow the procedure that is outlined on page 11.

- **Guess the flashcard.** Arrange the class into a circle. Show the toy and pet flashcards one by one and say *toy* or *pet*, as appropriate, each time. After a while, encourage the class to say the words while you remain quiet.
- Make a pile of the flashcards, all face down. Take one of them, look at it without anyone seeing. Say, e.g. *I've got a pet. It's big. It's black.* Encourage guesses using *Is it a …?* (e.g. *Is it a dog? Is it a cat?*)
- When your flashcard has been guessed ask a volunteer to take over your role. They choose a face down flashcard from the pile and say, e.g. *I've got a toy. It's big. It's yellow.*
- Continue, involving as many pupils as possible.

Ending the lesson

- Sing *Pluto's song* from Lesson 2. Encourage the class to do the actions and give different pupils turns at holding up the pet flashcards.
- Say *Goodbye* to the class.

Activity Book (Optional)

If you are using the *New Chatterbox* Activity Book, use page 28 now.

Match and write.

Pupils follow the leads from each speaker to the animal and complete the sentences in the speech bubbles with the names of the animals.

Unit 8 Extra activities

Hunt the pet

Language practised
What's this? It's a ... cat, dog, bird, fish, hamster, rabbit

Materials needed
Flashcards: *cat, dog, bird, fish, hamster, rabbit*

- Hide the pet flashcards around the room so that the pictures are not visible.
- Ask pairs of children to come out and find a hidden flashcard. When they have spotted one, one pupil in the pair asks *What's this?* The other pupil takes the flashcard and answers, e.g. *It's a fish*.
- Continue the process with other pairs.

Guess the pet

Language practised
Is it a ...? cat, dog, bird, fish, hamster, rabbit

Materials needed
Flashcards: *cat, dog, bird, fish, hamster, rabbit*
A blindfold

- Blindfold a volunteer and pass the pet flashcards round the class. Say *Stop* and choose one of the pupils with a flashcard. That pupil must make an appropriate noise for the pet on their flashcard. The rest of the class can join in.
- The blindfolded pupil asks questions, e.g. *Is it a hamster?* until they can make a definite guess, e.g. *It's a cat*.

In my bag

Language practised
I've got a ... in my bag, toys, pets, classroom items

Materials needed
A bag

- Hold up your bag and say *I've got a rabbit in my bag*.
- Prompt the next pupil to say *I've got a dog and a* (a toy, pet or classroom item of their choice) *in my bag*.
- The next pupil must repeat the whole sentence and add a pet, toy or classroom item of their own choice.
- Continue in the same way, helping each other out, until the sentence becomes too long for anyone to remember.

Lesson 1

Language focus
Food: *a sandwich, a sausage, an apple, an orange, a donut, an ice cream*
Identifying food

Classroom English
A / an, my favourite

Materials needed
Flashcards: *a sandwich, a sausage, an apple, an orange, a donut, an ice cream*

Starting the lesson

- Greet the class as usual. Ask a few individuals *How are you?*
- Review *I've got a ...* . Hold up a classroom item, e.g. a book and ask the class to continue *I've got a book*.
- Ask different pupils to hold up other classroom items and say, e.g. *I've got a pencil*.
- Sing the *I'm Pluto* song from Unit 8, Lesson 2.

Presentation

- Display the six food flashcards around the room.
- Point to each flashcard, say the word for the class to repeat. Use *a* or *an* as appropriate, but don't draw attention to this grammar point at this stage.
- Pass the flashcards around the class until you say *Stop*. Call out the food words. The pupils with the flashcards hold them up when they hear the words. Repeat this a few times involving as many pupils as possible.

Practice (PUPIL'S BOOK p. 54)

49 Listen, point and say.

- Say *Open your books* and show page 54. Explain that the children are planning to go on a picnic and have written a list of food they would like to have.
- Say *Listen, point and say*. Play the recording. Pupils listen.

  Tapescript
  Child: A sandwich, an apple, an orange, a sausage, a donut, an ice cream.

- Play the recording again and pause after each line. Pupils point to the correct food each time and repeat the word.
- Divide the class into six groups. Give a food flashcard to each group. Say the six food words in random order. Each group jumps up when they hear their word.

41

(50) Listen and draw.

- Show the empty frames along the bottom of the Pupil's Book page. Explain that the class will hear four food words. They should draw the food into the appropriate frame each time.
- Play the recording. Pause after each word to allow pupils time to draw a simple picture.

   Tapescript
   1. A sausage.
   2. An ice cream.
   3. An orange.
   4. A donut.

- When everyone is ready check the activity together. Call out each number (1–4) and ask the class to call out the food in that picture.

- **What's missing?** Arrange the class into a circle. Place the six food flashcards in the centre.
- Say each of the food words. The class pretends to eat that food.
- Say *Close your eyes*. Remove one of the cards. Say *Open your eyes*. As soon as the pupils realise which card is missing, they start pretending to eat that food. When everyone is miming, ask one pupil to say the food word.
- Continue in the same way.

(51) Story (PUPIL'S BOOK p. 55)

- Say *Open your books* and show page 55.
- Ask if the class can remember what happened in the eighth episode of the story, in Unit 8: Pluto picked up the same delicious donut smell in the park as he had smelt before and ran towards it with Zoko following. They reached a café which seemed to be empty but that is where the smells were coming from.
- Play the recording. The pupils follow in their books.

   Tapescript
   Zoko   Shh – listen, Pluto!
   Zoko   Let's hide!
   Doris Have you got the key, Hubert?
   Hubert Yes, Doris. I've got the key.
   Doris And I've got the chocolate chips.
   Hubert Mmm. Chocolate chip donuts – my favourite!
   Doris DJ? We're here, Joe!
   Zoko   They've got DJ!

- Ask if anyone can guess what *my favourite* means. Say the words for the class to repeat.
- Say Hubert's line *Mmm. Chocolate chip donuts – my favourite*, for the pupils to repeat.
- Change to *Ice cream – my favourite*. Pupils repeat.
- Play the recording again. Stop after each line and pupils repeat it, first chorally and then individually.

Story performance

- Ask three pupils to come to the front. Play the recording. The pupils act out the parts of Zoko, Hubert and Doris, supported by the recording. The rest of the class does the sound effects for Donut Joe clattering and cooking in the background and Pluto's barking and sniffing.
- If time allows, ask other groups of three to act out the episode.

Ending the lesson

- Go round the class saying a familiar word (e.g. a family member, a toy, a colour, a classroom item, a pet or food) to each pupil. Each pupil to whom you say a food word stands up.
- Continue until everyone is standing up and then say *Goodbye* to the class.

Activity Book (Optional)

If you are using the *New Chatterbox* Activity Book, use page 29 now.

Look and number.

Pupils look at the picture and write the number of each item of food in the correct box.

Find, circle and write.

Pupils look at the picture, find and circle the word and write it next to the line.

Lesson 2

Language focus
Have you got a / an ... ice cream, sausage, sandwich, orange, apple, donut?
Asking and answering about possession

Materials needed
Flashcards: *ice cream, sausage, sandwich, orange, apple, donut*

Starting the lesson

- Greet the class as usual.
- Hold up the six food flashcards. Pupils call out the words.
- Distribute the flashcards to six pupils. Ask the pupils with cards to hold them up and ask *What's this?* The class replies, e.g. *It's a sausage*.
- Continue the procedure, involving as many pupils as possible.

Presentation

- Distribute the food flashcards to six pupils. Then ask each of the pupils, e.g. *Have you got an ice cream? Have you got a sandwich?* The pupils answer *Yes* or *No*.

- Redistribute the flashcards and ask again. Encourage the rest of the class to join in with the answers.

Practice (PUPIL'S BOOK p. 56)

52 Listen, look and say.

- Say *Open your books* and show page 56. Say *Look and listen*. Explain that the class will hear the children asking each other what they have got in their picnic boxes.
- Play the recording.

   Tapescript
   Suzy: Have you got an orange?
   Sam: Yes.
   Sam: Have you got a donut?
   Suzy: No
   Zak: Hee hee!

- Play the recording again. This time pause after each question to allow the class to call out the answers.
- See if anyone realises why Suzy has so little in her picnic box. Draw attention to Zak running away with her food.

Look and write *yes* or *no*.

- Ask different pupils to read out Zak's speech bubbles at the bottom of the page.
- Ask other pupils to give the answers *Yes* or *No*. Then ask everyone to write the words onto the lines.
- Go round checking and helping.

53 Song (PUPIL'S BOOK p. 57)

- Say *Open your books* and show page 57.
- Play the recording of *Jelly Beans*. Pupils listen and look at the pictures.

   Tapescript
   Oranges and sausages,
   Apples and ice cream,
   Sandwiches and donuts,
   And a bag of jelly beans!

   Jelly beans, jelly beans
   Yellow, red and blue!
   Jelly beans, jelly beans –
   A bag for me and you!

- Give each child a sheet of paper. Ask them to draw one of the food items mentioned in the song.
- When they are ready, play the song again. Everyone sings along and holds up their picture as their food is mentioned.

Ending the lesson

- Place a food flashcard behind your back. Ask the pupils at one table or in one row to guess what you have got, e.g. *Have you got an orange?*

- If you answer *Yes* that group or row says *Goodbye* and moves towards the door. If you answer *No* they continue asking.
- Continue with a new flashcard and a new table or row, until everyone has said *Goodbye*.

Activity Book (Optional)

If you are using the *New Chatterbox* Activity Book, use page 30 now.

Match and draw.

Pupils draw a line from each object to the character it belongs to and draw the item into the picture.

Lesson 3

Language focus
Unit 9 revision

Function
Practising and consolidating the language

Materials needed
Flashcards: *a sandwich, a sausage, an apple, an orange, a donut, an ice cream*
Classroom items, ideally a bag of jelly beans

Starting the lesson

- Greet the class as usual. Ask *How are you?* to individuals. They reply *I'm fine, thank you*.
- Do a quick review of classroom items by asking everyone to put a selection of them on their desks.
- Ask different pupils, e.g. *Have you got a rubber?* If they have the item the pupil holds it up and answers *Yes*. If not, they answer *No*.
- Encourage volunteers to take over your role.

Practice (PUPIL'S BOOK pp. 58–59)

Draw.

- Say *Open your books* and show page 58. Explain that they should all choose familiar food to draw in the picnic box on the left (the one entitled *Me*).

Ask and answer. Then draw.

- Say *Let's work in pairs*. Explain that each pair will ask each other, e.g. *Have you got an apple?* If the answer is *Yes* they will draw an apple into the picnic box on the right, the one entitled *My friend*. To ensure they do not miss anything, each pupil should ask their partner about all six familiar food items.
- When they have finished they check with each other. Each pupil's picnic box marked *My friend* should have the same contents as their partner's picnic box marked *Me*.
- Ask a few individuals *Have you got a / an …?* questions about their own picnic boxes.

43

Look and write.

- Show the class the crossword on page 58. Explain that they should write the word for each picture, following the direction of the arrow.
- Go round checking and helping.

Look, circle and write.

- Ask individuals to read the speech bubbles under each picture on page 59. The rest of the class helps the reader to decide which adjective or colour and food word to choose.
- Ask everyone to circle the appropriate words in each speech bubble.
- When everyone is ready, say *Write*. Everyone draws a familiar food of their choice on the empty plate and then completes the sentence in the speech bubble.
- Go round checking and helping.

My English is …

Follow the procedure that is outlined on page 11.

Guess the flashcard.

- Arrange the class into a circle. Show the toy and pet flashcards one by one and say *toy* or *pet*, as appropriate, each time. After a while encourage the class to say the words while you remain quiet.
- Make a pile of the flashcards, all face down. Take one of them, look at it without anyone seeing. Say, e.g. *I've got a pet. It's big. It's black*. Encourage guesses using *Is it a …?* (e.g. *Is it a dog? Is it a cat?*)
- When your flashcard has been guessed ask a volunteer to take over your role. They choose a face down flashcard from the pile and say, e.g. *I've got a toy. It's big. It's yellow*.
- Continue, involving as many pupils as possible.

Ending the lesson

- Sing the *Jelly Beans* song from Lesson 2. If you have been able to get any jelly beans, distribute these and encourage pupils to hold up the yellow, red and blue ones when they appear in the song (before they eat them!).
- Say *Goodbye* to the class.

Activity Book (Optional)

If you are using the *New Chatterbox* Activity Book, use page 31 now.

Complete the questions and circle *Yes* or *No*.

Pupils complete each question with the correct word from the box. When the questions are complete, they look at Zak's picnic box and circle *Yes* if he has the food and *No* if he does not have it.

Unit 9 Extra activities

Guess the food

Language practised
Is it a / an …? sausage, sandwich, apple, orange, ice cream, donut

Materials needed
Flashcards: *sausage, sandwich, apple, orange, ice cream, donut*

- Choose a food flashcard and hold it up, with its back to the class. Ask *What's this?* Encourage guesses, e.g. *Is it an apple? Is it a donut?*
- When someone guesses correctly, show them the card and ask them to take over your role.

My picnic

Language practised
I've got a … for my picnic, sausage, sandwich, apple, orange, ice cream, donut

Materials needed
Picnic box

- Hold up your picnic box and say *I've got an apple for my picnic*.
- Prompt the next pupil to say *I've got an apple and* (a food of their choice) *for my picnic*.
- The next pupil must repeat the whole sentence and add another food of their choice.
- Continue in the same way, helping each other out, until the sentence becomes too long for anyone to remember.

 (PUPIL'S BOOK p. 60)

Extra language
It's very … Count the …

Materials needed
A large backing sheet, glue or sticky tape

(54) Listen and complete.

- Say *Open your books* and show page 60. Allow pupils time to look at the photos and make comments on differences or similarities to their own pets.
- Play the recording. Pupils listen.
  Tapescript
  Jenny: I've got a cat. It's brown.
  Ben: I've got a rabbit. It's grey.
- Read the speech bubbles slowly. Pupils follow in their books. Pause at the gaps and see if the class can supply the pets and the colours.
- Ask volunteers to read each speech bubble again. The rest of the class points at the correct photo.

Make a class pet picture

- Encourage pupils to bring in photos of their pets, or to draw pictures of them.
- Have ready a large backing sheet and ask the pupils to stick their pictures or photos onto the sheet to make a big attractive collage.
- While they are doing this, prepare large speech bubbles to stick around the collage, e.g. *Count the birds, Have you got a fish? Count the dogs. I've got a hamster.*
- When the collage is ready, gather the pupils round it and invite everyone to say or ask something about it, using the speech bubbles as a guide.

End the lesson

- Explain that you are going to ask everyone what pet they have. Anyone who does not have a pet can pretend to have one.
- Call out a pet, e.g. *rabbit*. Anyone who has (or is pretending to have) a rabbit puts up their hand and says (individually) *I've got a rabbit*. The pupils with rabbits then all go towards the door,
- Continue until everyone is at the door, then say *Goodbye* to the whole class.

Activity Book (Optional)
If you are using the *New Chatterbox* Activity Book, use page 32 now.

Read and match.
Pupils look at the picture of all the children with their pets. Then they read the sentences and draw a line between each sentence and the corresponding picture.

✓, draw and write.
Pupils draw items of food onto the tray and tick the boxes next to the words of the items they have drawn.

Revision time! (PUPIL'S BOOK p. 61)

Play the game.

- Say *Open your books* and show page 61. Ask individuals to name the items in the circles.
- Make sure everyone knows where to find the stickers for the game – in the sticker insert in the middle of the book.
- Arrange the class into pairs or small groups. Explain how to play the game.
  1 Start at the start sign and throw a dice.
  2 Count round the course according to the number you throw.
  3 Name the item or colour in the circle you land on. If you say the word correctly (your partner or other group members or your teacher will say if it is correct) find the corresponding sticker and stick it on.
  4 Take turns to throw until you have landed on all the circles and have covered them all with stickers. Once you have been round once, carry on round again and again.

Test
Ask pupils to do Test 3

Lesson 1

Language focus
Faces: *head, eyes, ears, mouth, nose, hair*
Identifying parts of the face

Classroom English
What colour is?

Materials needed
Flashcards: *colours, head, eyes, ears, mouth, nose, hair*
Classroom items

Starting the lesson

- Greet the class as usual. Ask a few individuals *How are you?*
- Hold up a selection of classroom items and ask *What's this?* and *What colour is it?* about each item.
- Sing the *Jelly Beans* song from Unit 9, Lesson 2.

Presentation (PUPIL'S BOOK p. 62)

56 Listen, point and say.

- Point to your hair, eyes, ears, mouth, nose and finally your whole head. Say the word each time. The class copies you and repeats the word each time.
- Say the words. The class points but you remain still.
- This time you point at a part of your face, encourage the class to say the right word.
- Say *Open your books* and show page 62. Tell them they are going to hear a chant about the parts of the face. Play the recording.

Tapescript

Anna, Sam, Suzy, Robocat,	Mouth, head, eyes, ears, nose,
Zak and Zeeky:	hair.

- Say *Stand up*. Play the recording again. The class points to the parts of their faces as they hear the chant.
- Divide the class into smaller groups. Ask each group to come and do a performance of the chant. They can add as much movement as they like as long as they are still pointing to the appropriate parts of the face as the words occur in the chant.

57 Listen and draw.

- Show the pictures along the bottom of the Pupil's Book page and ask volunteers to say which features are missing.
- Explain that the class will hear the numbers *1–4* and a part of the face. They should draw in the named part of the face each time.
- Play the recording. Pause after each word so that the pupils have time to draw the part of the face.

Tapescript
1 eyes
2 nose
3 mouth
4 hair

- Check the activity together by drawing four empty faces on the board, numbered 1–4. Ask volunteers to name and draw the missing feature for each face.

- **Touch your face.** Ask the class to *Stand up*. Explain that you will ask them to touch a part of their face. They must do this quickly as whoever is last will sit down.
- Say, e.g. *Touch your eyes*. Everyone touches their eyes. Allow a little practice time before asking the pupil who is last each time to sit down.
- If you wish you can introduce a new rule: the pupils should only carry out your instruction if you add *please*. Anyone who makes a mistake, or does the actions when you did not say *please*, must sit down.

58 Story (PUPIL'S BOOK p. 63)

- Say *Open your books* and show page 63.
- Ask if the class can remember what happened in the ninth episode of the story, in Unit 9: Pluto and Zoko have realised that Donut Joe is in the little café. Is he being kept a prisoner by Doris and Hubert, to make donuts for them?
- Play the recording. The pupils follow in their books.

Tapescript

Zoko	It's DJ! He's in the kitchen!
Doris	Here, Hubert – 3 of DJ's donuts.
Hubert	Oh, great! Thanks, Doris!
Zoko	Poor Pluto! You're all wet!
Pluto	Woof.
Zoko	Are you hungry, Pluto? Here – have a nice battery.
Pluto	Mmm. Woof.
Zoko	Mmm. I'm hungry!

- Ask the class why Zoko is offering Pluto a battery? (Zoko, being an electric robot, sees electric batteries as delicious food.)
- Read the line *Have a nice battery* for the class to repeat. Encourage individuals to pretend to offer food to each other, saying, e.g. *Have a nice donut. Have a nice sandwich* etc.

Unit 10

Story performance
- Ask three pupils to come to the front. Play the recording. The pupils act out the parts of Zoko, Hubert and Doris, supported by the recording. The rest of the class does the sound effects for Donut Joe clattering and cooking in the background and Pluto's miserable whimpering in the background.
- If time allows, ask other groups of three to act out the episode.

End the lesson
- Ask the class to *Stand up*. Play a quick round of *Touch your face*. This time as pupils are out, they say *Goodbye* and move towards the door.

Activity Book (Optional)
If you are using the *New Chatterbox* Activity Book, use page 33 now.

Match.
Pupils draw a line from each word to the correct feature.

Look and write.
Pupils look at each picture and write the name of the feature which has just been added to the face.

Lesson 2

Language focus
He's / She's got ... a / an (adjective) (colour) mouth, nose, eyes, ears, face, hair
Describing others

Materials needed
Classroom items, a funny mask (these are usually available in toy shops, or they can easily be made by attaching a piece of elastic to a paper plate, cutting eye holes, drawing on a mouth, sticking on one section of an egg box painted red for a nose and wool for hair), paper plates, egg boxes, paint, wool, elastic

Starting the lesson
- Greet the class as usual.
- Do a quick review of parts of the face saying, e.g. *Touch your hair, touch your ears,* etc.
- Point to your eyes and say, e.g. *I've got brown eyes*. Encourage others to do the same, saying *I've got blue / green / brown / grey eyes*.

Presentation
- Ask a girl volunteer to wear the funny mask. Say, e.g. *She's got a red nose*. The class repeats.
- Encourage other comments, e.g. *She's got black hair, she's got a red mouth*. Check they are using *She's got* each time.
- Ask a boy volunteer to wear the mask. Say, e.g. *He's got a red nose* and ask the class to tell you the difference (*He's*). It is worth focusing on this as children can find it hard to remember and if they get it right from the start it will be much easier for them later.
- Repeat the procedure with a few different boys and girls wearing the mask and other pupils giving comments.

59 Practice (PUPIL'S BOOK p. 64)
Listen, point and say.
- Say *Open your books* and show page 64. Say *Listen, point and say*. The class should point to the feature being described each time
- Play the recording.
  Tapescript
  Suzy: She's got pink ears.
  Anna: He's got a big nose.
- Play the recording again. This time pause after each line to allow the class to repeat.
- Invite further comments *She's got ...* and *He's got ...* comments about Zeeky and Sam.

Look and write.
- Ask different pupils to read the sentences about Zak at the bottom of the page.
- Ask other pupils to suggest ideas for the missing words. Then ask everyone to write the words onto the lines.
- Go round checking and helping.

- **Make a mask.** Demonstrate making a mask. Attach the two ends of a piece of elastic to a paper plate, cut eye holes, draw on a mouth, paint one section of an egg box red for a nose and stick it on, add wool for hair.
- Distribute the materials for making masks to each group or table.
- As pupils are making their masks, go round asking questions, e.g. *Have you got a blue nose?* etc. They answer *Yes* or *No*.
- When they are ready they all put on their masks. Ask different pupils to comment about their neighbour, e.g. *She's got blue hair, she's got a big yellow nose* etc.

Unit 10

Song (PUPIL'S BOOK p. 65)
- Say *Open your books* and show them page 65.
- Play the recording of *Sam the spider*. The pupils listen and look at the pictures.

Tapescript
I've got long, black legs
And a big, hairy nose,
I've got 6 yellow eyes
And 8 hairy toes.

I'm Sam the Spider!
Ho! Ho! Ho!

He's got long, black legs
And a big, hairy nose,
He's got 6 yellow eyes
And 8 hairy toes.

He's Sam the Spider!
Ha! Ha! Ha!

- Ask a group of children to be Sam the spider. Play the song again. The group playing Sam joins in with his words and demonstrates his long legs, big nose, eyes and toes.
- Everyone else sings along with the rest of the song.
- Swap the groups so that everyone has a chance to be Sam.

Ending the lesson
- Ask everyone to pick up a classroom item. Now ask each pupil to say what their neighbour has got, e.g. *He's got a book, She's got a pencil case*.
- Ask the class, e.g. *Have you got a rubber?* Everyone with a rubber holds it up and says *Yes*. They move towards the door and say *Goodbye*.
- Continue until everyone has said *Goodbye*.

Activity Book (Optional)
If you are using the *New Chatterbox* Activity Book, use page 34 now.

Number.
Pupils number the story pictures in the same order they appear in the Pupil's Book.

Lesson 3

Language focus
Unit 10 revision

Function
Practising and consolidating the language.

Materials needed
Flashcards: colours, *eyes, ears, mouth, nose, hair*
Classroom items, real toys (e.g. a car, a ball, a doll, a guitar, a teddy bear)

Starting the lesson
- Greet the class as usual. Ask *How are you?* to individuals. They reply *I'm fine, thank you*.
- Do a quick review of colours by handing round the flashcards and asking everyone to call out what they have got, e.g. *I've got yellow*.
- Redistribute the flashcards and repeat the procedure.

Practice (PUPIL'S BOOK pp. 66–67)
Read, join and say.
- Say *Open your books* and show page 66. Describe one or two of the robots saying, e.g. *He's got green hair, She's got purple ears*. The pupils find and point to the robots which fit your descriptions.
- Say *Let's work in pairs*. Explain that the pupils in each pair will take turns reading the sentences and finding the robots. They draw lines from each sentence to the robot it describes.
- Go round checking and helping. Make up some new sentences for a few individuals and see if they can find the robots you are describing.

Look and write.
- Show the class the pictures of Zak and Zeeky on page 67. Before reading the sentences, ask individuals to say, e.g. *He's got a book, She's got a teddy bear*.
- Go through the sentences orally asking pupils to supply the missing words, then ask them to write the words on the lines.
- Go round checking and helping.

My English is ...
Follow the procedure that is outlined on page 11.

Ending the lesson
- Sing the *Sam the spider* song, from Lesson 2. Again, ask a group of pupils to be Sam and to sing his lines.
- Say *Goodbye* to the class.

Activity Book (Optional)

If you are using the *New Chatterbox* Activity Book, use page 35 now.

Read and colour.

Pupils read the sentences and colour Zeeky's mask as described.

Complete the sentences and circle *Yes* or *No*.

Pupils complete the sentences, then look at the pictures and circle *Yes* if the sentence is true or *No* if it is not. Remind pupils that *She* describes the girl and *He* describes the boy.

Unit 10 Extra activities

I've got, He's got

Language practised
I've got ..., *He's / She's got ...*, toys, classroom items, food, pets

Materials needed
Flashcards: toys, classroom items, food, pets

- Ideally arrange the class in a circle. Distribute the flashcards.
- Ask a volunteer to hold up their flashcard and say, e.g. *I've got a hamster*. They then choose another pupil and say, e.g. *He's got a ball*.
- The pupil with the ball holds up their card and says *I've got a ball* and then they choose the next pupil. This keeps everyone concentrating as no-one knows when they will be chosen.

My mum / dad / brother / sister

Language practised
Family members
He's / She's got ...

- Ask everyone to draw a picture of someone in their family.
- When they are ready, ask individuals to describe their picture, saying, e.g. *This is my dad. He's got black hair, he's got a red mouth, he's got brown eyes*.

My face

Language practised
I've got green eyes, small ears, a big pink mouth ...

- Say, e.g. *I've got a pink mouth*.
- Prompt the next pupil to say *I've got a pink mouth and* (*green eyes* – or something else of their choice).
- The next pupil must repeat the whole sentence and add another feature of their choice.
- Continue in the same way, helping each other out, until the sentence becomes too long for anyone to remember.

Lesson 1

Language focus
Clothes: *a T-shirt, a skirt, socks, a jumper, trousers, shoes*

Classroom language
Put on your ..., Well done!

Materials needed
Flashcards: colours, *a T-shirt, a skirt, socks, a jumper, trousers, shoes*

Start the lesson

- Greet the class as usual.
- Do a quick review of colours. The pupils pass round the colours flashcards until you say *Stop*. Everyone with a flashcard holds it up. The class calls out the colours.
- Repeat the procedure but this time the pupils holding the cards hold them up and call out the colours.

Presentation

- Hold up the clothes flashcards, one by one, saying the word each time. The class repeats.
- Say each of the new words again, pointing to the article of clothing on yourself or on a pupil each time. The pupils do the same.
- Say each word but this time remain still and allow the pupils to point.

Practice (PUPIL'S BOOK p. 68)

61 Listen, find and say.

- Say *Open your books* and show page 68. Explain that Suzy is packing to go and stay overnight with her friend, Anna. She has made a list of the clothes she wants to take. Zeeky is supposedly helping her find the clothes, but she is actually removing everything from the bag.
- Say *Listen, find and say*. Play the recording. Pause after each article of clothing for the pupil to repeat the word and find the clothing in the picture.

Tapescript
Suzy a T-shirt, a skirt, socks, a jumper, trousers, shoes

Say *Let's work in pairs*. One pupil in each pair calls out the clothes on the list and the other pupil finds them in the picture. They can call them out in random order if they want to challenge their partner a little more.

- Go round listening and helping.

62 Listen and circle.

- Show the pictures at the bottom of the page. Ask volunteers to say the clothing words.
- Explain that the class will hear the word for one of the pictures in each pair. They should circle the correct picture.
- Play the recording. Pause after each word to give pupils time to circle the picture.

Tapescript
1 socks
2 a skirt
3 shoes
4 a T-shirt

- Check the activity by saying the numbers *1–4* and asking volunteers to draw the circled picture on the board each time. The class says the correct word.

Listen and colour.

- Explain that the class will hear another recording. This time each article of clothing will be preceded by a colour. They should colour each picture according to what they hear.
- Play the second part of the recording. Pause after each line to give pupils time to colour the picture.

Tapescript
1 black trousers
  blue socks
2 a pink skirt
  a yellow T-shirt
3 black shoes
  white socks
4 a purple jumper
  a red T-shirt.

- Hand out the colour and clothes flashcards. Play the second part of the recording again. Pause after each line. The children with the correct colour and clothes flashcards hold them up each time.
- Go round checking and helping with any misunderstandings.

- **Put on your clothes.** Ask everyone to stand up. Say *Put on your shoes* and prime a pupil to demonstrate miming putting on their shoes. Say *Put on your shoes* to the class. They all mime putting on their shoes.
- Continue the procedure with *Put on your socks / skirt / jumper / T-shirt / trousers*.
- Once everyone is confident, play it as a game. The last pupil to start doing the appropriate mime sits down.

Unit 11

Story (PUPIL'S BOOK p. 69)
- Say *Open your books* and show page 69.
- Ask if the class can remember what happened in the tenth episode of the story in Unit 10: Doris came out of the café to give Hubert a plate of donuts. Pluto was so excited by the delicious smell and sniffed so enthusiastically that the barrel of water he had been balancing on collapsed, and Pluto got soaked – but he has spotted Donut Joe through the window.
- Play the recording. The pupils follow in their books.

Tapescript

Zoko	Listen, Luke: Donut Joe is here!
Luke	Are you at the park, Zoko?
Zoko	Yes – we're at the Lake Café.
Luke	Wait for Captain Shadow, Zoko.
Captain Shadow	Is Donut Joe here?
Zoko	Yes, Captain. Listen!
Captain Shadow	Have you got the number for the Lake Café, Chocolate Chip?
Chocolate Chip	Yes – I've got it here …
Captain Shadow	Good! Let's try it: 0 – 7 – 9 – 8 – 6 – 4 – 2

Story performance
- Ask four pupils to come to the front. Play the recording. The pupils act out the parts of Luke, Zoko, Captain Shadow and Chocolate Chip, supported by the recording. The rest of the class does the sound effects for the motorcycle, Donut Joe clattering and cooking in the background and the telephone ringing.
- If time allows, ask other groups of four to act out the episode.

Ending the lesson
- Play a number memory game. Say a series of three and then four numbers, for the class to repeat back to you. Increase the length of the list of digits and challenge the class to remember them.
- Challenge rows or tables of pupils to say a series of digits and then say *Goodbye*.
- Continue until you have said *Goodbye* to everyone.

Activity Book (Optional)
If you are using the *New Chatterbox* Activity Book, use page 36 now.

Read and draw.
Pupils copy and draw the items shown in the panel in the correct frame.

Complete the crossword.
Pupils look at the clues and complete the crossword to find the mystery word in the tinted boxes.

Draw and write.
Pupils draw the mystery object in the box and write the word for it.

Lesson 2

Language focus
He's / She's got …a / an (adjective) (colour) T-shirt, skirt, jumper, trousers, shoes, socks
Describing other people's clothes

Materials needed
Real T-shirts, skirts, jumpers, trousers, shoes, socks

Starting the lesson
- Greet the class as usual.
- Do a quick review of clothes saying, e.g. *Touch your shoes, touch your T-shirt* etc.
- Point to something you are wearing and say, e.g. *I've got a blue skirt, I've got black shoes*. Encourage others to do the same.

Presentation
- Ask a volunteer to describe someone in the class, e.g. *She's got a red T-shirt, green trousers and brown shoes*.
- Encourage other comments, e.g. *She's got black hair, she's got a red mouth*. Check they are using *She's got* each time.
- Ask volunteers to guess who it is using *Is it (name)?* When someone has guessed correctly they choose someone to describe for the rest of the class to guess.

Practice (PUPIL'S BOOK p. 70)

Read, join and say.
- Say *Open your books* and show page 70. Say *Read, join and say*. Ask individuals to read the descriptions.
- Say *Let's work in pairs*. Each pair looks closely at all the descriptions and decides which pictures they fit.
- When they have decided they draw a line from each of the two descriptions to the pictures they fit.
- Ask volunteers to read out the two descriptions.

Read, colour and write.
- Read the two sentences slowly. The pupils follow the lines in their books.
- Explain that they are now going to complete the drawings of the girl and the boy with the items of clothing mentioned in the sentences (trousers and a jumper for the boy, a skirt and a T-shirt for the girl).

- When they are ready they colour the clothes and then write the colour words on the lines.
- Go round checking and helping.

- **Secret pictures.** Hand a sheet of paper to each pupil. Show them how to fold the paper over and then over again, into thirds.
- Demonstrate drawing a head on the top third of the paper. Start the outline of a neck and then fold the top third away so that only the bottom of the neck is visible. Then demonstrate drawing the top part of a body, wearing a jumper or T-shirt. Fold this part of the paper away so that only the top part of the legs are visible. Then demonstrate drawing a skirt or trousers, socks and shoes.
- Explain that everyone is going to draw a head and the top of the neck then pass on their paper to the next pupil. They draw the top part of a body on the next piece of paper and then pass this on. They then draw the legs on this piece of paper and pass this on.
- Everyone then opens a completed picture and colour all the clothing. They then show and describe the picture to the rest of the class, e.g. *He's got a green T-shirt, red trousers and blue shoes.*

- (64) **Song** (PUPIL'S BOOK p. 71)
- Say *Open your books* and show page 71.
- Play the recording. The pupils listen and look at the pictures.
  Tapescript
  He's got dancing trousers
  She's got a dancing skirt
  I've got a dancing jumper
  And a dancing red T-shirt …

  And we've all got dancing socks.
  Dancing socks! Dancing socks!
  We've all got dancing socks -
  Dance, dance, dance!
- Hand out the clothes flashcards. Play the song again. The pupils with flashcards hold them up as they are mentioned in the song. Everyone else points to their own clothing at the right moments.

Song performance

- Divide the class into smaller groups. Ask each group to prepare a dance routine for the song. Give them time to do this and then ask as many groups to perform their routines as time allows.

Ending the lesson

- Call out colours and items of clothing, e.g. *white socks, a red jumper*. Any pupils wearing these jumps up and moves towards the door.
- Continue until everyone is at the door and then say *Goodbye*.

Activity Book (Optional)

If you are using the *New Chatterbox* Activity Book, use page 37 now.

Colour and circle *Yes* or *No*.

Pupils colour in the story episode in the same colours that are on the Pupil's Book page. Then they look at the sentences and circle *Yes* or *No*, depending on whether the sentence is correct or not.

Lesson 3

Language focus
Unit 11 revision

Function
Practising and consolidating the language.

Materials needed
Flashcards: clothes, parts of the face

Starting the lesson

- Greet the class as usual. Ask *How are you?* to individuals. They reply *I'm fine, thank you*.
- Do a quick review of parts of the face. Hand out the flashcards and call out, e.g. *hair*. Everyone touches their hair and the pupil with the hair flashcard holds it up.
- Redistribute the flashcards and repeat the procedure.

Practice (PUPIL'S BOOK pp. 72–73)

Look and write A or S.

- Say *Open your books* and show page 72. Read out the names of Anna and Suzy. Read the first sentence and encourage the class to look and see which girl the description fits.
- Say *Let's work in pairs*. Explain that the pupils in each pair will take turns reading the sentences and identifying the girl. They write the first letter of their name on the line after each sentence.
- Go round checking and helping. Make up some new sentences for a few individuals and see if they can identify the correct girl.

🔊 Listen and play.

- Show the class the clothes pictures at the bottom of the page. Explain that everyone will choose six of the pictures and place counters (or small pieces of paper) on them.
- Play the recording. Whenever a pupil hears one of the clothes on which they placed a counter, they remove that counter. The first pupil to remove all their counters puts up their hand.

Tapescript
White socks
A purple skirt
Black shoes
A blue T-shirt
Brown trousers
Pink socks
A green skirt
A red jumper
A yellow T-shirt
Grey trousers

Draw a friend and colour.

- Ask everyone to draw a picture of a friend or family member. They should be wearing a jumper or a T-shirt and looking happy but apart from that the pupils have freedom to draw what they want.

Circle and write.

- When the pupils have finished their pictures, ask volunteers to read the sentences. Explain that everyone will fill in the gaps and choose the words to fit their pictures.
- Go round checking and helping, and ask individuals to read out their sentences.

My English is …

Follow the procedure that is outlined on page 11.

- **Mystery descriptions.** Arrange the class into a circle. Describe a pupil, e.g. *She's got a blue T-shirt* (you may need to add another feature if lots of pupils are wearing blue T-shirts!).
- The pupil referred to jumps up and it is now their turn to describe someone else, e.g. *He's got green trousers and brown shoes.*
- Again, the pupil being described jumps up and then describes someone else.

Ending the lesson

- Sing the *Dancing socks* song from Lesson 2. Again, ask groups of pupils to show their dance routines to the rest of the class.
- Say *Goodbye* to the class.

Activity Book (Optional)

If you are using the *New Chatterbox* Activity Book, use page 38 now.

Read and colour.

Pupils read the description and colour the boy and girl's clothes as described.

Circle *He's got* or *She's got*.

Pupils look at the pictures and circle *He's got* if it is a boy or *She's got* if it is a girl to complete the sentences.

Unit 11 Extra activities

Drawing dictation

Language practised
He's / She's got … colours, parts of the face, clothes

Materials needed
Sheets of paper for each pupil

- Give each pupil a sheet of paper. Explain that you will read out a description and that they should draw and colour what you describe.
- Give a description, e.g. *She's got brown hair and blue eyes. She's got a red T-shirt, yellow trousers and brown shoes.*
- Ask pupils to show their finished drawings, then repeat the procedure.

My clothes

Language practised
I've got … (clothes)

- Say, e.g. *I've got a purple jumper.*
- Prompt the next pupil to say *I've got a purple jumper and* (*grey trousers* – or something else of their choice).
- The next pupil must repeat the whole sentence and add another article of clothing of their choice.
- Continue in the same way, helping each other out, until the sentence becomes too long for anyone to remember.

Lesson 1

Language focus
Furniture: *bed, table, sofa, TV, box, chair*
Identifying items of furniture

Classroom English
(Name and name) *are my friends*

Materials needed
Flashcards: *1–10, bed, table, sofa, TV, box, chair*

Starting the lesson

- Greet the class as usual. Ask a few individuals *How are you?*
- Review numbers *1–10*. Start by counting from 1–10 round the class.
- Hold up number flashcards in random order. Each time, the pupil identifies the number and then counts from 1 up to that number.
- Sing the *Dancing socks* song, from Unit 11, Lesson 2. Ask a group of pupils to lead the rest of the class in their dance routine.

Presentation (PUPIL'S BOOK p. 74)

66 Listen, point and say.

- Hold up the flashcards for *bed, table, sofa, TV, box, chair*. Say the word each time. The class repeats the word each time.
- Show the flashcards. Say the words. The class points to the correct flashcard each time.
- Say *Open your books* and show page 74. Explain that we are looking at the Anna and Sam's house. Can the pupils spot Anna, Suzy, Sam, Zak and Zeeky?
- Say *Listen, point and say*. Play the recording. The class finds and points to the items of furniture they hear and repeats the words each time.

Tapescript
Bed, box, sofa, TV, table, chair.

67 Listen and complete.

- Show the beginnings of pictures along the bottom of the Pupil's Book page.
- Explain that the class will hear Zak and Zeeky asking about the pictures.
- Play the recording. Pause after each word so that the pupils have time to complete the picture according to what Zak and Zeeky say.

Tapescript
1. Zeeky	What's this?	
Zak	It's a TV.	
2. Zak	What's this?	
Zeeky	It's a table.	
3. Zeeky	What's this?	
Zak	It's a chair.	
4. Zak	What's this?	
Zeeky	It's a sofa.	
5. Zeeky	What's this?	
Zak	It's a bed.	
6. Zak	What's this?	
Zeeky	It's a box.	

- Check the activity together by calling out numbers 1–6. Ask volunteers to say the item of furniture each time. Check any misunderstandings.
- **Go to the table.** Place a chair, a table and a box in separate places in the classroom. Display the flashcards of the *TV*, *sofa* and *bed* in other places.
- Explain that you are going to ask groups of pupils to, e.g. *Go to the bed*. They must all go and stand by the flashcard of the bed.
- Then ask the group to go somewhere else, e.g. *Go to the box*. Continue, gaining speed as the pupils gain confidence.
- Then allow another group to have a turn.

68 Story (PUPIL'S BOOK p. 75)

- Say *Open your books* and show page 75.
- Ask if the class can remember what happened in the eleventh episode of the story, in Unit 11: Zoko called in Captain Shadow, to help rescue Donut Joe. She arrived on her motorcycle and called the café on her mobile to see if Donut Joe would answer.
- Play the recording. The pupils follow in their books.

Tapescript

Doris	Who's this?
Doris	Hello?
Captain Shadow	Hello. It's Captain Shadow here. Is Donut Joe with you?
Doris	Yes, he's here.
Donut Joe	No, I'm not missing! I'm fine! Hubert and Doris are my friends.
Donut Joe	I've got special donuts for Chocolate Chip's birthday!
Chocolate Chip	Oh, thanks, DJ – your donuts are great!
Pluto	Woof! Woof! Woof!
Zoko	Donuts? No, thanks – I've got batteries! Mmm!

- Check that everyone understands that Donut Joe was not being kept a prisoner and that he was helping Hubert and Doris prepare lots of secret donuts for Chocolate Chip's birthday.
- Ask the class what they think *Hubert and Doris are my friends!* means. Encourage volunteers to say, e.g. (Name and name) *are my friends*.
- Play the recording again. Stop after each line and pupils repeat it, first chorally and then individually.

Story performance
- Ask five pupils to come to the front. Play the recording. The pupils act out the parts of Zoko, Captain Shadow, Chocolate Chip, Donut Joe and Doris, supported by the recording. The rest of the class does the sound effects for the motorcycle, Pluto's barking, and Zoko eating a battery.
- If time allows, ask other groups of five to act out the episode.

End the lesson
- Place the six furniture flashcards around the room. Ask small groups of pupils to, e.g. *go to the TV / box / table*. They then move towards the door.
- Do the same for other groups until everyone is at the door. Then say *Goodbye* to all the class.

Activity Book (Optional)
If you are using the *New Chatterbox* Activity Book, use page 39 now.

Look and number.
Pupils look at the picture and write the number of the piece of furniture in the correct box.

Look and write.
Pupils look at each silhouette and decide what it is. They complete the sentence with the name of the item of furniture.

Lesson 2

Language focus
Where's the ...? in / on
Furniture: *bed, table, sofa, TV, box, chair*
Asking about where things are; using prepositions of place

Classroom language
Put the ... on / in the ...

Materials needed
Flashcards: *bed, table, sofa, TV, box, chair*, a real box with a lid or flaps so that items can be placed on it, classroom items, a box template for each child (copied onto card or thick paper), scissors, glue or sticky tape

Starting the lesson
- Greet the class as usual.
- Do a quick review of items of furniture by saying the words and asking the class to make up a mime (e.g. sleeping for *bed*, opening a box for *box*, sitting for *chair* etc.)
- Ask the class to pass round the furniture flashcards. When you say *Stop*, the pupils with the flashcards hold them up and say the words.

Presentation
- Have a box ready. Prime a pupil to put a book inside the box. Look puzzled and say *Where's the book?* Encourage the reply *In the box.*
- Now prime a pupil to put the book on top of the box. Ask *Where's the book?* Encourage the reply *On the box.*
- Repeat the procedure with other classroom items. Involve as many pupils as possible.

Practice (PUPIL'S BOOK p. 76)

69 Listen and say.
- Say *Open your books* and show page 76. Say *Listen and say*. Play the recording. The pupils follow in their books.

Tapescript
Sam Where's the hamster?
Anna In the box.

Anna Where's the hamster?
Suzy On the bed.

- Play the recording again. This time pause after each question for the class to answer.

Look and write *in* or *on*.
- Ask volunteers to read Zak and Zeeky's questions.
- Say *Let's work in pairs*. Ask the pairs to look at the pictures and decide together whether *in* or *on* is needed in each answer.

- Check the activity by asking pairs to read out the question and answer for each picture.

Rap (PUPIL'S BOOK p. 77)
- Say *Open your books* and show them page 77.
- Play the recording for *Ants! Ants!* The pupils listen and look at the pictures.

Tapescript
Ants on the table,
Ants on the chairs,
Ants in the cupboard,
Ants on the stairs!

Ants on the sofa,
Ants in my bed,
Ants on the TV,
Ants on my head!

- See if pupils can identify the *cupboard* in the picture but don't spend too much time on this extra vocabulary.
- Divide the class into smaller groups. Ask each group to decide on actions or mimes for each of the places or items of furniture mentioned in the rap.
- Play the rap again for them to practise chanting along and doing their actions.

Rap performance
- Ask the groups to perform the rap, with the actions they have agreed, to the rest of the class, supported by the recording.
- While they watch each performance, encourage the rest of the class to beat time by tapping their feet, or using any percussion instruments available.

Ending the lesson
- Ask the class to tidy up, asking, e.g. *Put the pencils in the pencil case, Put the pens in the box, Put the books on the table*.
- When everyone has helped put things where you have asked, say *Thank you* and *Goodbye*.

Activity Book (Optional)
If you are using the *New Chatterbox* Activity Book, use page 40 now.

Find and circle 8 differences.

Pupils look at the two pictures and find and circle eight differences. Encourage children to tell you what the differences are.

Lesson 3

Language focus
Unit 12 revision

Function
Practising and consolidating the language

Materials needed
Flashcards: *skirt, T-shirt, jumper,* pets, toys

Starting the lesson
- Greet the class as usual. Ask *How are you?* to individuals. They reply *I'm fine, thank you*.
- Distribute flashcards on chairs, tables and in boxes (but still visible) around the classroom.
- Ask, e.g. *Where's the rabbit? Where's the skirt? Where's the guitar?* Encourage answers such as *In the box* or *On the table*.
- Demonstrate making a whole sentence, e.g. *The cat is on the chair*. Ask volunteers to do the same.

Practice (PUPIL'S BOOK pp. 78–79)

Look and join.
- Say *Open your books* and show page 78. Start by asking questions about the picture, e.g. *Where's the bird? Where's the donut?*
- Now encourage volunteers to make whole sentences about the picture, e.g. *The hamster is in the car*.
- Demonstrate drawing lines to link the words to make whole sentences about the picture. Ask the class to continue doing this. Go round checking and helping.
- Check the activity by asking pupils to read out their sentences.

Ask and answer.
- Point to the bottom of the page, where Zak and Zeeky are looking up at the picture and asking each other questions about it.
- Ask two pupils to read their speech bubbles aloud. In pairs, pupils can then ask and answer questions about the picture.

Play and say.
- Draw a simple 5 x 5 grid on the board, with numbers 1–5 down the left side and 6–10 along the bottom and colours outlining the rows.
- Give a reference, e.g. *1, 8* and ask a pupil to come and draw a cross in the correct square. Repeat this until you feel the class is confident about how to find a grid reference.
- Show the class the *Play and say* activity on page 79. Ask a pupil to read Zak's speech bubble *3, 10*. Ask everyone to find the correct box and give the answer (Zeeky's bubble) *It's a green chair*.

- Call out more references for the class to find, each time giving the answer *It's a ...* .
- Ask pupils to give grid references for the rest of the class to find.
- Say *Let's work in pairs*. Pupils in each pair take turns giving a grid reference and finding the correct box (*It's a ...*).
- Go round listening and helping.

My English is ...

Follow the procedure that is outlined on page 11.

Ending the lesson

- Chant the *Ants! Ants!* rap from Lesson 2. Again, ask groups of pupils to show their dance routines while the rest of the class claps to the rhythm.
- Say *Goodbye* to the class.

Activity Book (Optional)

If you are using the *New Chatterbox* Activity Book, use page 41 now.

Match and write *in* or *on*.

Pupils read the questions and look at the picture to find the answers. They draw a line from each question to the correct answer and complete the sentence with *in* or *on*.

Unit 12 Extra activities

Musical flashcards

Language practised
All vocabulary

Materials needed
A random selection of the flashcards – the same number as there are pupils in the class

- Clear a large space in the middle of the classroom. Lay the flashcards face down on the floor.
- Play some music. The pupils dance around the room until you stop the music. Then they go and pick up a flashcard.
- Ask three individuals to say the word for the picture on their flashcards. These flashcards are removed from the game.
- Everyone else replaces their flashcards. The three pupils without flashcards leave the game and watch from the side. The rest of the pupils dance around the room again.
- Continue the procedure until there is only one player left.

What's in the box?

Language practised
Toys, classroom items, pets, clothes, food, *in the box*

Materials needed
Flashcards: toys, classroom items, pets, clothes, food
A box

- Put a selection of ten flashcards in a box. Ask *What's in the box?* Take out the flashcards one by one. Ask volunteers to say the words. Spread out the flashcards so that everyone can have a good look, then replace them in the box.
- Ask *What's in the box?* See if the class can remember all ten flashcards. Write the words on the board as pupils say them.
- Change the selection of flashcards and play again.

What's missing?

Language practised
All Starter level vocabulary

Materials needed
All flashcards

- Clear a large space in the middle of the classroom. Lay a selection of about ten flashcards face up on the floor.
- Give the class time to look at all the flashcards, then ask them to close their eyes as you remove one.
- Ask them to open their eyes. Can anyone name the missing flashcard?
- Repeat the procedure several times with different flashcards.

Units 10-12

 (PUPIL'S BOOK p. 80)

Extra language
This is my home, I'm from … England, Scotland, Northern Ireland, Wales

Materials needed
A large map of the United Kingdom, a map of the pupils' country, a large backing sheet, glue or sticky tape

 **Listen, read and colour.**

- Say *Open your books* and show page 80. Allow the pupils time to look at the photos and make comments on differences or similarities to their own homes.
- Point to the map of the United Kingdom on the page (if you have a larger version use that). Explain that the United Kingdom is made up of four countries: England, Scotland, Northern Ireland and Wales. The Queen rules over all four countries. The rest of the island called Ireland is an independent country.
- Say the names of the four countries again. The pupils point to each country as you say it on the central map on the page.
- Play the recording. The pupils follow in their books and point to the right photo and the right country each time.

  Tapescript
  I'm David. I'm from England. I'm 8. This is my home.
  I'm Calum. I'm 7. I'm from Scotland. This is my home.
  I'm Erin. I'm from Northern Ireland.
  I'm Rosy. I'm 6. I'm from Wales.

- Ask different pupils to read each speech bubble. The rest of the class point again
- Play the recording again, pausing after each speech bubble. This time pupils refer to the central map as a guide and colour the relevant part of each corner map according to the country mentioned in the corresponding speech bubble.
- Check the activity together by reading the speech bubbles again and asking pupils to point to the correct country on your map.

Display board. Ask individuals to write speech bubbles saying, e.g. *I'm from Hungary*. Explain that if anyone originates from another country they can write that in their speech bubble if they want to.

- Stick the large sheet with the outline of the pupils' country onto the display board. Ask individuals to cut out their speech bubbles and stick them on the board.

End the lesson
- As this is the end of the last lesson of the Starter level, ask the class to look back through their books and find their favourite page. When they are ready, ask volunteers to hold open their book at the right page and say the English words for some of the pictures.
- Say *Goodbye* to the class.

Activity Book (Optional)
If you are using the *New Chatterbox* Activity Book, use page 42 now.

Look and ✓ or ✗.
Complete the sentences.

Pupils look at the pictures of the bedrooms and tick the items of furniture on the list in each room. Then they complete the descriptions of the rooms.

Draw and write.

Pupils draw a picture of their own bedroom and complete the sentence describing it.

 (PUPIL'S BOOK p. 81)

Play the game.

- Say *Open your books* and show page 81. Ask individuals to name the items in the circles.
- Make sure everyone knows where to find the stickers for the game – in the sticker insert in the middle of the book.
- Arrange the class into pairs or small groups. Explain how to play the game.
  1 Start at the start sign and throw a dice.
  2 Count round the course according to the number you throw.
  3 Name the item or colour in the circle you land on. If you say the word correctly (your partner or other group members or your teacher will say if it is correct) find the corresponding sticker and stick it on.
  4 Take turns to throw until you have landed on all the circles and have covered them all with stickers. Once you have been round once, carry on round again and again.

Test
Ask pupils to do Test 4.

Festivals

 Halloween! (PUPIL'S BOOK p. 82)

Language focus
Ghost, witch, cat

Materials needed
A folded sheet of card for each pupil, a narrow strip of card for each pupil, glue or sticky tape, dressing up clothes for a witch (e.g. witch's hats), old sheets for ghosts, face paints for cats

Start the lesson

- Explain that Halloween means the evening before All Saints' (All Hallows) Day. People believed that evil spirits etc. came out for a party on Halloween before they were purged away on All Saints' Day, the next day.
- Children in many countries like to dress up as witches, ghosts, witch's cats etc. and have parties at Halloween. They also carve faces on pumpkins and put night lights inside them to shine in the dark.

73 Listen and say.

- Say *Open your books* and show page 82. Ask the class what they think is happening (the children are dressed up for a Halloween party). Point out the pumpkins on the table.
- Play the recording. The pupils follow in their books.
  Tapescript
  I'm a witch. Hee, hee!
  I'm a ghost. Wooh!
  I'm a cat. Miaow!
- Divide the class into three groups, one for the cat, one for the witch and one for the ghost. Practise each group's line with them.
- Play the recording again. This time each group joins in with their character's lines.
- Encourage individuals to dress up in the witch's hats, or wrap themselves in the sheets for ghosts, or to have their faces painted as cats. They should say, e.g. *I'm a ghost Wooh!*

Make a ghost card.

- Show the pictures of the ghost card. Read through the instructions on the page and demonstrate making the card as follows:
1 Draw a ghost. Cut it out.
  Draw a simple ghost on a piece of paper and cut it out.
2 Fold a strip of paper again and again.
  Concertina-fold a thin strip of card to make a sort of spring.
3 Stick the ghost in the card.
  Stick the ghost picture onto the top end of the folded strip of card. Stick the other end of the folded card onto the middle of the inside page of the folded card.
- Write a speech bubble saying *Happy Halloween* and stick this onto the front page of the card. Open the card and show the ghost popping up.
- Hand out a piece of paper, a folded sheet of card and a narrow strip of card to each pupil.
- Go round helping them make their cards. Encourage them to say *Happy Halloween* when they give their cards to their families or friends.

74 Listen and sing.

- Show the class the chant at the bottom of the page. Ask volunteers to read the words.
- Play the recording. The class joins in.
  Tapescript
  Miaow! Miaow!
  What's that?
  Miaow! Miaow!
  It's a cat.

  Wooh! Wooh!
  Is that you?
  Hee! Hee!
  Yes, it's me.
- Divide the class in half, one half are cats and the other half are ghosts. The cats join in with the *Miaows* in the first verse and the questions in the second verse. The ghosts join in with the questions in the first verse and the *Woohs* and *Hee Hees* in the second verse.
- If the class is confident, ask them to do the chant without the support of the recording. Encourage them to put lots of expression into it.

End the lesson

- Encourage everyone to choose whether they are a ghost, a witch or a cat. (If there is time they could dress up or have their face painted.)
- They go round the room saying, e.g. *Miaow! I'm a cat!*
- Say *Stop!* Then say, e.g. *Goodbye, ghosts*. All the ghosts say *Goodbye* in ghostly voices and make their way to the door.
- Continue until everyone is at the door.

Activity Book (Optional)

If you are using the *New Chatterbox* Activity Book, use pages 43 and 44 now.

Match.

Pupils draw a line from each speech bubble to the correct speaker.

Find and count.
Pupils look at the picture and count the number of each animal or object. You can choose whether to teach *bat*, *pumpkin* and *spider*.

Colour.
Pupils look at the key and colour each area the colour indicated to complete the picture. When they have finished, ask the children what they can see in the picture.

Christmas (PUPIL'S BOOK p. 83)

Language focus
Happy Christmas! star, ball, Christmas tree, present

Materials needed
A circle of paper for each pupil, scissors OR lots or strips of coloured paper, sticky tape, coloured pens, glitter, if possible a very small present for each pupil, e.g. a pencil, a notebook or a small sweet

Start the lesson
- Ask the class what they know about the festival of Christmas. How do they celebrate it?

🎧 Listen and say.
- Say *Open your books* and show page 83. Ask the class what they think is happening (the girl in the picture is about to go into her house which is decorated for Christmas).
- Play the recording. The pupils listen to Jenny's speech bubble. Then they listen to and repeat the Christmas words.
  Tapescript
  Jenny   Come and see our Christmas tree.
  Younger sister   Here's a present!
- Say *Let's work in pairs*. Ask the class to find the items shown in the box. Each time they find one of the items they should point to it and say to their partner, e.g. *Here's a star*.
- Go round listening and checking.

Make a snowflake.
- Show the pictures of the snowflake. Read through the instructions on the page and demonstrate making the snowflake as follows:
  1 Fold the paper.
  Fold a circle of paper in half, then again in half, then again in half.
  2 Cut the paper.
  Demonstrate making small cuts along the folded edges and the curved edges of the folded paper.
  3 Open the paper.
  Open out the paper to show how it resembles a snowflake.
- Hand out a paper circle and scissors to each pupil. Go round encouraging them and helping where necessary.
- When they have cut the snowflake they can decorate them with coloured pens and glitter.
- Display the snowflakes around the classroom.

🎧 Listen and sing.
- Ask the class to try reading the lyrics of the song before you play the recording. (Once they have worked out one line, the rest will be easy!)
- Play the recording. Everyone joins in.
  Tapescript
  We wish you a merry Christmas!
  We wish you a merry Christmas!
  We wish you a merry Christmas
  And a Happy New Year!
- Divide the class into three groups. Each group joins in with one of the first three lines, then everyone joins in with the last line as loudly as they can.
- Give a performance of the song to parents or other children in the school.

End the lesson
- Hand each pupil a small present. Ask them to give these to each other saying *Happy Christmas* as they do so.
- Say *Goodbye* and *Happy Christmas* to the whole class.

Activity Book (Optional)
If you are using the *New Chatterbox* Activity Book, use pages 45 and 46 now.

Draw.
Pupils draw the correct number of stars, balls and presents next to or on the Christmas tree to complete the picture. They may like to colour the tree too.

Draw some more Christmas things.
Pupils draw a picture of something they do on Christmas Day.

Colour and ✓ the things you do at Christmas.
The pictures show six things that happen at Christmas in a typical English home. Picture 1 shows children carol singing – it is traditional for groups of children and adults to visit their neighbours and sing carols (Christmas hymns) in the weeks before Christmas. Picture 2 shows a girl hanging up her stocking – all children hang up a stocking at the end of their bed on Christmas Eve. Father Christmas secretly visits during the night and fills the stocking with small presents for the child to find in the morning. Picture 3 shows the family opening their

presents from under the tree. Picture 4 shows the girl eating Christmas dinner – roast turkey, roast potatoes and vegetables. Picture 5 shows the girl about to cut the Christmas cake. Picture 6 shows the family pulling the crackers which is done at dinner or tea time. Inside the cracker is a hat, a joke and a very small present. Compare the English Christmas with Christmas in your country and pupils colour and tick the pictures which show activities which are done in your country.

 Easter! (PUPIL'S BOOK p. 84)

Language focus
Chocolate, eggs

Materials needed
A paper plate, a length of elastic and card for ears for each pupil, cotton wool (local equivalent), small round chocolate sweets (e.g. chocolate buttons), small chocolate eggs or similar small chocolates for everyone

Start the lesson

- Ask the class what they know about the festival of Easter. How do they celebrate it?

77 Listen, read and match.

- Say *Open your books* and show page 84. Ask the class what they think is happening (the children are showing each other what they've received for Easter). Play the recording. Then ask volunteers to read the speech bubbles.
  Tapescript
  I've got a chocolate rabbit.
  I've got a chocolate egg.
- The rest of the class point to the rabbit and the eggs as they are mentioned.

Make a rabbit mask.

- Show the pictures of the rabbit mask. Demonstrate making the mask as follows:
  1 Punch a hole on either side of a paper plate. Tie the two ends of a length of elastic around the holes.
  2 Make eye holes in the plate.
  3 Draw on a mouth.
  4 Cut ears from card and stick these onto the plate.
  5 Stick cotton wool (local equivalent) all over the plate leaving a hole for a chocolate nose.
  6 Attach a round chocolate sweet (e.g. a chocolate button or similar) for a nose.
- Help the class make their rabbit masks. When they are ready encourage them to put on the masks and say *I'm a chocolate rabbit*.

78 Listen and sing.

- Show the rap at the bottom of page 84. Play the recording. The pupils follow the words.
  Tapescript
  I'm a chocolate rabbit,
  I've got 10 chocolate toes,
  I've got big chocolate ears,
  And a small chocolate nose.
- Encourage the class to join in the rap and wear their rabbit masks. Ask smaller groups to take turns giving performances.

End the lesson

- Hide enough small chocolates around the classroom for each pupil to have one. Before you do this, check that no-one in the class is allergic to chocolate. Encourage the class to find them. Each time someone finds one for themselves, they can help another pupil find one.
- Say *Goodbye* and *Happy Easter* to the class.

Activity Book (Optional)

If you are using the *New Chatterbox* Activity Book, use page 47 now.

Draw the path.
Number the eggs.

Pupils draw the path through the maze from the Start to the Easter basket. On the way they number the Easter eggs 1–10 in the order they pass them. Note: It is traditional for English children to hunt for chocolate Easter eggs or rabbits on Easter Day, in their house or in the garden.

Colour the eggs.

Pupils look at the key and colour each egg they have numbered in the correct colour.

Special needs

Fast finishers

In any class, there are pupils who work more quickly than the others and complete a task before the rest of the class have finished. The activities below can be used to give 'fast finishers' an additional challenge or consolidation activity. Alternatively, you may have pupils in the class who are capable of learning more language than is presented in the Pupil's Book. If you would like to teach more vocabulary, you can use the illustrations to expand their knowledge. Simply point to two or three extra items in the pictures and say the words. In some units it might be more appropriate to extend the language by including a new structure, or by combining the target structure with a previously learned one.

A list of possibilities for further language for each unit is given below.

Unit 1   *What's your name?*
Unit 2   Numbers *11–20*
Unit 3   *aunt, uncle, grandma, grandpa, cousin*
Unit 4   *What colour it is? It's …*
Unit 5   *How old is he / she? He / She's …*
Unit 6   *Is it (colour)? Yes, it is / No, it isn't*
Unit 7   *tall, short, young, old*
Unit 8   *horse, cow, sheep*
Unit 9   Focus more on *a / an*
Unit 10 *arms, legs, hands, feet*
Unit 11 more clothes
Unit 12 more household items
         under, behind

Extra activities for fast finishers

The following activities require the pupils to write the target vocabulary:

- Say a topic or word set to the pupil, for example *Colours* and a number, for example, *six colours*. The pupil writes six colours, for example, *red, blue, yellow, green, white, black*. Alternatively, ask them to write down as many as they can.
- Ask a pupil to look around the classroom and write down as many objects or colours as they can.
- Ask a pupil to write a list of the items they can name in their bedroom.
- Give a pupil a list of words and ask them to write the opposites, for example, *black – white, happy – sad*.
- Ask the pupils to draw a picture and label the items in the picture, e.g. an imaginary monster or a classroom and write sentences about the picture.
- Ask individual pupils to make a wordsquare for a friend using six words from a particular page. Make sure the pupil writes the hidden words to find under the grid.
- Write a sentence on a piece of paper, for example, *I've got a dog*. Ask the pupil to write three more sentences of the same type. If there is more than one pupil doing the task, they can write simple questions for each other.

The following activities require the pupils to draw or write numbers to confirm their understanding of written or spoken English:

- Write a list of six objects or animals on a piece of paper and ask the pupil to draw each object or animal.
- Divide a page into ten sections. Label each section with a colour word and ask the pupils to colour each section in the appropriate colour.
- Ask pairs of pupils to dictate a list of numbers to each other. (They will need to keep a record of the list.) The other pupil writes down the numbers.
- Dictate a simple sentence to the class, e.g. *She's got a teddy bear and a guitar*. The pupils draw a picture to illustrate the sentence.

Activities for dyslexic children

Dyslexic children have more difficulty than most when trying to recognise, form and order letters. By practising and focusing on problem letters and relating sounds to letters, these difficulties can be overcome. The activities in this section offer ideas on how to help dyslexic children when learning English.

Visual recognition of letters

Some children have difficulty distinguishing between the letters they see. The following activity focuses on distinguishing between two letters which have a similar appearance, e.g. *b* and *d*, *p* and *q*, *a* and *d*, *h* and *n* etc.

Letter challenge

Aim: To help pupils distinguish particular letters. This can be tailored to the needs of each pupil.

- Draw a simple picture of a river with lots of stepping stones. Each stone should be big enough to write a letter on. Make a copy of the picture for each pupil.
- Choose two letters you would like to practise. Write these letters in the stepping stones. Give the page to the pupils and tell them to trace over one letter in red and the other letter in blue. They can then draw lines between all the stones containing the same letter to cross the river.

Point to the letter

Aim: To practise visual letter recognition.

- You will need a set of alphabet cards. Put some letter cards on the floor or the wall. Say and show the pupils a letter and ask them to point to the correct card.

Sound and letter identification

Some children have difficulty identifying sounds and then relating the sound they hear to the appropriate letter. The following activities first practise aural recognition of sounds and then relate them to letters

Matching sounds

Aim: To help pupils identify sounds.

- Read the script. Ask the pupils to repeat the initial sound at the beginning of each line. The children jump up or raise their hand when they hear the word beginning with the focus sound.

Script

Matching sounds and letters.

1	p [puh] (pupils repeat)	red	blue	pink
2	d [duh] (pupils repeat)	dad	mum	brother
3	c [kuh] (pupils repeat)	cat	school	bag
4	s [suh] (pupils repeat)	sister	Zak	Zeeky
5	b [buh] (pupils repeat)	bag	dad	dog
6	g [guh] (pupils repeat)	bike	robot	guitar
7	t [tuh] (pupils repeat)	teddy bear	cat	doll

Finding the letter

Aim: To help pupils identify the appropriate letter for a sound.

- Give the pupils a copy of the following list of words:

1	rubber	pen	book
2	dad	brother	sister
3	white	red	yellow
4	ball	doll	guitar
5	hamster	rabbit	cat
6	apple	orange	ice cream

- Say the following sounds. The pupils circle the word which starts with the letter relating to the sound they hear:
  1 /p/
  2 /d/
  3 /w/
  4 /b/
  5 /r/
  6 /o/

Word formation

Some children have difficulty ordering letters within words correctly.

Ordering letters

Aim: To build words using alphabet cards.

- Write a simple consonant–vowel–consonant word on the board, for example, cat or dog. Give a pupil the same set of letters and ask them to put them in the right order.
- When they can do this confidently, say a word, give the pupils the letters but do not write the word on the board.

Jump through a word

Aim: To use movement as way of reinforcing the order of letters within a word.

- Place the alphabet cards for a simple word across the floor in a random order. Say the word. Ask a pupil to jump from one letter to the other in the correct order. Children that are watching can chant the letters as the pupil jumps from one to another.

Games

Board and Paper Games
Noughts and crosses
Draw a 3 x 3 grid on the board. Number the squares 1–9 and stick a flashcard face down in each square. Divide the class into two teams, the Os and the Xs. The teams take turns to choose a square. When a team has chosen a square, turn the picture over and ask them to name the item. If they get the answer right, draw an O or an X in the square. If they get the answer wrong, stick the picture back face down. Either team can choose this square again. The aim of the game is to get three Os or Xs in a row – horizontally, vertically or diagonally.

Guessing Games
Picture puzzle
Start drawing a picture on the board. Draw it in stages and let the pupils take turns to guess what it is by asking, for example, *Is it a ball?* Invite the pupil who guessed correctly to the front of the class. Show them a picture but make sure the rest of the class cannot see it. The pupil draws the picture on the board. The rest of the class guesses what it is.

Magic bag
You need an empty bag for this game. Show the bag to the class and tell them it is a magic bag. Cast a magic spell over the bag then pretend to pull out something, for example, *a pencil* or *a rubber*. Mime what you would do if you had this object in your hands. The pupils guess what you have pulled out of the bag by saying, for example, *It's a rubber*. Invite the pupil who guessed correctly to the front of the class and let them try pulling an invisible object out of the bag.

Memory Games
Burglar
Put eight objects or flashcards on your table. Let the pupils look at the items for a few moments. Then ask them to close their eyes while you remove an object or picture. The pupils then look again and try to see which object has been taken.

All change
Say the name of a topic or word set, for example *Numbers*, and encourage the pupils to count around the class. When they reach *10*, say *All change, Colours*. Continue around the class with each child saying a colour. If anyone gets stuck, encourage another child to help by pointing to a colour. After a while say *All change* again and give them a new word set, for example, *Animals*.

Action and Mime Games
Word race
Draw a line down the centre of the board, dividing it in half. Invite two pupils to the front and give them each a marker pen or piece of chalk. Say a noun or number and tell the pupils to draw the object or write the number on their side of the board. When you have about ten numbers or pictures on the board, divide the class into two teams.
Call out the names of one member from each team and say, for example, *the pencil, six,* etc. The two players must run to the board and circle the correct picture or number in their half of the board. The first player to do so gets a point for their team. Rub out the circles and continue until everyone has had a go.

The mime game
Stand in front of the class and mime what you would do if you had a particular object in your hands, for example, write with a pencil or put on your shoes. The pupils take turns to guess what it is. Invite the pupil who guesses correctly to the front of the class. Tell the pupil what object to mime using and let the rest of the class guess what it is.

Please
Prepare a set of commands for the pupils to carry out, for example *Sit down, Stand up* etc. Give the instructions to the whole class. If you finish with the word *please*, they should perform the action. If you miss out the word *please*, the children should not do what you have told them. Any child who performs the action when you have not said *please* is out.

Assessment

Test Tapescripts

Test 1

Activity 1 Listen and circle.
Example This is my dad.
1 This is my mum.
2 This is my sister.
3 This is my brother.
4 This is my dad.
5 This is my mum.

Activity 2 Listen and tick or cross.
Example Hello!
1 Listen.
2 Stand up.
3 Open your book.
4 Look.
5 Goodbye.

Activity 3 Listen and draw.
Example a bag
1 a pen
2 a rubber
3 a pencil case
4 a book
5 a pencil

Test 2

Activity 1 Listen and match.
Example
    Adult   How old are you?
    Girl   I'm four.
1   Adult   How old are you?
    Boy   I'm eight.
2   Adult   How old are you?
    Boy   I'm six.
3   Adult   How old are you?
    Girl   I'm seven.
4   Adult   How old are you?
    Boy   I'm ten.
5   Adult   How old are you?
    Girl   I'm five.

Test 3

Activity 1 Listen and number.
Example 1 I've got a cat.
2 I've got a hamster.
3 I've got a dog.
4 I've got a bird.
5 I've got a rabbit.
6 I've got a fish.

Test 4

Activity 1 Listen and colour.
Paul's got a grey jumper.
He's got black trousers.
He's got brown shoes.
Fiona's got an orange T-shirt.
She's got a pink skirt.
She's got blue socks and shoes.

Answer Key

Test 1

Activity 1
1 mum
2 sister
3 brother
4 dad
5 mum

Activity 2
1 ✗
2 ✓
3 ✓
4 ✗
5 ✓

Activity 3
Check that pupils have drawn the correct item.

Activity 4
4 books
3 pencil cases
5 pencils
1 bag
2 rubbers

Test 2

Activity 1
1 8
2 6
3 7
4 10
5 5

Activity 2
1 a bike
2 a car
3 a teddy bear
4 a guitar
5 a doll

Activity 3
1 green – ball
2 blue – bag
3 red – car
4 yellow – teddy bear
5 brown – guitar

Activity 4
Bike 1 – grey
Bike 2 – purple
Bike 3 – yellow
Bike 4 – pink
Bike 5 – orange
Bike 6 – white

Test 3

Activity 1
dog – 3
fish – 6
rabbit – 5
bird – 4
cat – 1
hamster 2

Activity 2
1 She's big.
2 He's thirsty.
3 He's sad.
4 She's hungry.
5 She's happy.

Activity 3
1 Check that pupils have drawn a plate with a donut on it.
2 Check that pupils have drawn a lunch box with a sandwich and an apple.
3 Check that pupils have drawn a lunch box with a sausage and an orange in it.

Activity 4
1 Yes
2 No
3 No
4 Yes
5 Yes

Test 4

Activity 1
1 T-shirt – orange
2 trousers – black
3 skirt – pink
4 socks – blue
5 shoes – Paul/brown, Fiona/blue

Activity 2
1 hair
2 eyes
3 ears
4 nose
5 mouth

Activity 3
1 No
2 Yes
3 No
4 Yes

Activity 4
1 in the box
2 on the table
3 in the bed

Test 1 — Units 1–3

Name: _____ Score: ____ /20

1 🔊(19) **Listen and circle.**

/5

2 🔊(20) **Listen and tick ✓ or cross ✗.**

/5

Test 1

3 🎧 **Listen and draw.**

4 Find, count and match.

book   pen   pencil case   pencil   bag   rubber

6

5

Test 2   Units 4–6   Name: _____   Score: ____ /20

1 🎧 **Listen and match.**

___
5

2 **Look and circle.**

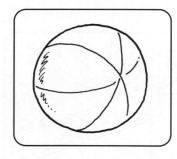   a teddy bear
   (a ball)

   a bike
   a teddy bear

   a bike
   a car

   a guitar
   a ball

   a car
   a doll

   a doll
   a guitar

___
5

68 PHOTOCOPIABLE © Oxford University Press • New Chatterbox Starter

Test 2

3 Find and colour.

black
1 green
2 blue
3 red
4 yellow
5 brown

4 Look and colour.

1 = grey   2 = purple   3 = yellow   4 = pink   5 = orange   6 = white

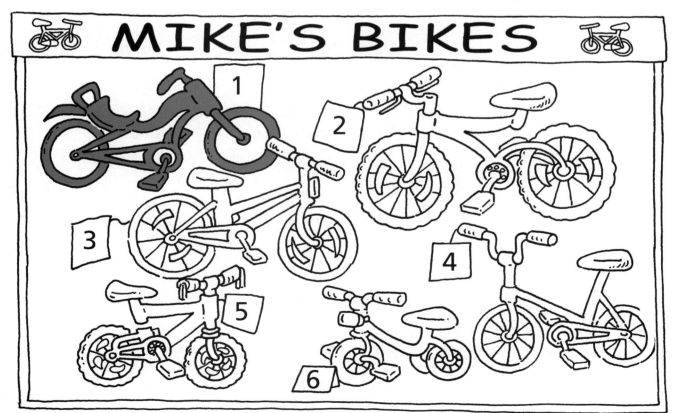

Test 3 — Units 7–9

Name: _____ Score: ____ / 20

1 🔊 **Listen and number.**

2 **Circle the correct word and match.**

	(He's) / She's	big
1	He's / She's	happy.
2	He's / She's	small.
3	He's / She's	hungry.
4	He's / She's	sad.
5	He's / She's	thirsty.

70 PHOTOCOPIABLE © Oxford University Press • New Chatterbox Starter

Test 3

3 **Read and draw.**

4 **Look and write Yes or No.**

Have you got an ice cream?   No.
Have you got a dog?   Yes.
1 Have you got an apple?   _____ .
2 Have you got an orange?   _____ .
3 Have you got a cat?   _____ .
4 Have you got a sandwich?   _____ .
5 Have you got a guitar?   _____ .

Test 4 Units 10–12   Name: _____   Score: ___ /20

1 Match. 🎧 Listen and colour.

  jumper
1 T-shirt
2 trousers
3 skirt
4 socks
5 shoes

Paul   Fiona

/5

2 Find and write.

   n b h e a d x   head

1    p h a i r l n   _____

2   e y e s m s o   _____

3   y u e a r s c   _____

4   g k w n o s e   _____

5   d m o u t h i   _____

/5

Test 4

3 Look and circle Yes or No.

	She's got black hair.	Yes	~~No~~
1	She's got red trousers.	Yes	No
2	She's got a big jumper.	Yes	No
3	She's got a white T-shirt.	Yes	No
4	She's got a small box.	Yes	No

4

4 Circle and write.

| the box | ~~the chair~~ | the table | the bed |

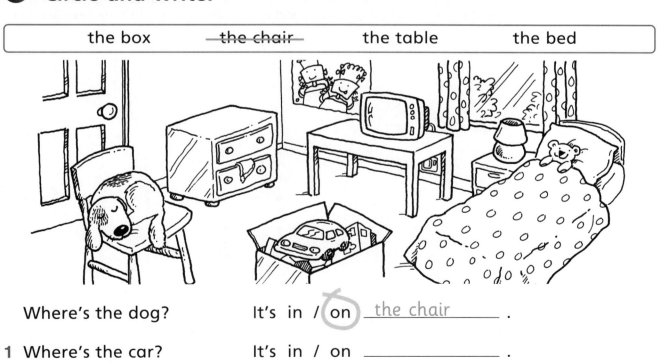

	Where's the dog?	It's in / ~~on~~ _the chair_ .
1	Where's the car?	It's in / on _____ .
2	Where's the TV?	It's in / on _____ .
3	Where's the teddy bear?	It's in / on _____ .

6

Assessment

Portfolio Teaching Notes

Now I can say ...

On these pages there are one or two statements relating to each book unit. You will need to give each pupil a copy of this page after finishing every three units of the Pupil's Book. After doing each revision section in the Pupil's Book and the test for that section (every three units), pupils should be asked to look at this page. They should read the statements for the three units they have just covered and decide if they are now confident that they can do those things in English (you may need to discuss the statements with the class first in their mother tongue). If they are confident, then they colour in the robot character for that statement. If they are fairly confident, but still a little unsure, they should colour in just the character's speech bubble and return to that statement after the next three units, when they have had more opportunity to revise and practise that language. If they don't think they can do it at all, they should leave it blank and revisit it after the following three units. This page should be revisited after completing units 3, 6, 9 and 12.

Dossier

This year I have ...

This page should be completed by each pupil at the end of the year. They should look back at all the project work they have done over the year, fill in the record and evaluate which piece was their best piece of work. Empty lines have been left for them to add in details of any extra projects you may have done, e.g. made puppets for the puppet theatre.

End of year review

This page should also be completed at the end of the year. Pupils look back through their books and decide which were their favourite songs, games, characters, stories, and projects and write some new words they have learned.

Portfolio

Now I can say ...

Portfolio

Portfolio

Dossier: This year I have …

Project	Date
made a class picture	
made a chart to show the class's age	
made a class pet collage	
done a project about countries in the UK	
made a ghost card for Halloween	
made a Christmas decoration	
done a survey about pets	
made a rabbit mask for Easter	

My best piece of work this year was: _____
_____
_____

Portfolio

End of year review

My favourite New Chatterbox song / chant is

_____.

My favourite New Chatterbox episode is

_____.

My favourite New Chatterbox project is

_____.

My favourite New Chatterbox game is

_____.

My favourite New Chatterbox story character is _____.

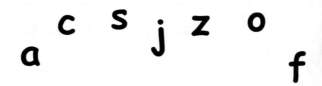

My favourite new word from New Chatterbox is _____ .

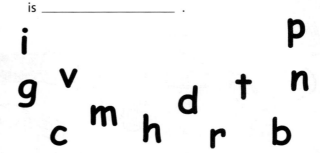

Wordlist

Unit 1
Hello
Hi
Goodbye
I'm ...
Stand up
Sit down
Open your book
Close your book
Look
Listen

Unit 2
Numbers 1–10
What's this?
It's a ...
bag
pen
pencil
rubber
pencil case
book

Unit 3
This is my ...
mum
dad
sister
brother
Who's this?
My ...

Unit 4
white
green
yellow
black
red
blue
How old are you?
I'm ...
Happy Birthday!

Unit 5
What's this?
It's a ...
ball
car
teddy bear
doll
bike
guitar
Is it a ...?
Yes
No

Unit 6
purple
brown
pink
orange
grey
What colour is it?
It's ...

Unit 7
I'm ...
You're ...
He's ...
She's ...
big
small
hungry
thirsty
sad
happy

Unit 8
hamster
rabbit
cat
dog
bird
fish
I've got a ...
It's ...

Unit 9
a sandwich
a sausage
an apple
an orange
a donut
Have you got a / an ...?
Yes
No

Unit 10
head
eyes
ears
nose
mouth
hair
He's got ...
She's got ...

Unit 11
T-shirt
jumper
skirt
shoes
socks
trousers
He's got ...
She's got ...

Unit 12
bed
table
chair
sofa
box
Where's the ...?
(It's) in ...
(It's) on ...

CERTIFICATE OF EXCELLENCE

This is to certify that

_____

has successfully completed New Chatterbox Starter _____

at _____ School

in

_____

Congratulations!

Signed: _____

Date: _____